Blerim Burjani

Election in Western Balkan and Policy

Blerim Burjani

Election in Western Balkan and Policy

E Political System

Dictus Publishing

Imprint

Cover image: www.ingimage.com

Publisher:
Dictus Publishing
is a trademark of
International Book Market Service Ltd., member of OmniScriptum Publishing Group
17 Meldrum Street, Beau Bassin 71504, Mauritius
Printed at: see last page
ISBN: 978-613-7-35572-5

INSTITUTI I KOSOVES PER POLITIKA ZHVILLIMORE (IKPZH)

BLERIM BURJANI

ELECTION IN WESTERN BALKAN AND POLICY

PRISTINA , 2021

BLERIM BURJANI

ELECTION IN WESTERN BALKAN AND POLITICAL DEVELOPMENT

Email:instiuti_politik@yahoo.com
Number of telephone +38344502546

Pristina

2021

Abbreviations

AAK-Alliance for Future of Kosovo

CEC-Central Election Commission

LDK-Democratic League of Kosovo

PDK-Democratic Party of Kosovo

VV-Self-determinant Movement

EP-European Parliament

EU-Europe Union

ECAP-Administrative Organ for Complain

PSD-Social Democratic Party

Content:

CHAPTER ONE

Executive summary

Political Development in Kosovo

The elections in Kosovo are a result of the political situation created in Kosovo after the Prime Minister's resignation, the reasons for the resignation were not due to an invitation sent by Prime Minister Haradinaj but the resignation was due to the US and EU requesting to abolish taxes on Serbian goods, and this had not been accepted by Haradinaj, which led to the extraordinary elections in Kosovo. Haradinaj had also made a platform for dialogue with Serbia that was not taken seriously neither in Kosovo nor in Brussels, a document that was more work-related to what should be dealt with in the Kosovo-Serbia negotiations and without detail. A law was later drafted for dialogue which was rejected by the Constitutional Court which decision addressed powers to negotiate to the Government and did not go large, PDK aware that Thaci will be deprived of the right to represent Kosovo in negotiations with Serbia, has been forced the government of state to resign. The elections were organized without prior reform of the election law, all issues remain the same. Kosovo needs reform in two respects:
legal and technical, so these two reforms should happen as soon as possible, but that did not happen, the elections were organized by the current law and with the same trouble. The voter list was not cleared from dead citizen , which remains the biggest concern.

- The conditional vote should be abolished
- Municipal Election Commissions should be depoliticized
- Polling stations should be depoliticized
- Central Election Commission should also be fully depoliticized
- Division of electoral zone should be done soon is possible.
- A new law should be issued for the political party
- Political parties must be registered in the courts
- Political parties working in contravention of the state constitution should be removed from the political activity register
- All votes must be counted at polling stations and only diaspora votes will have to be counted at the Ballot Counting Center.
- The law on transparency of political party donations should be issued by Parliament of Kosovo

- 40,000.00 thousand invalid votes in October 2019 by-elections

- 45% of citizens have voted in the October 2019 snap elections

- Political parties compline : ECAP decision-making regarding complaints of political entities and candidates for MPs after the announcement of the final results of the elections of 06 October 2019The Election Complaints and Appeals Panel - ECAP, announces public opinion that, by 10:50 today, has decided on all appeals filed by political entities and candidates for deputies that have been filed after the results of the election have been announced and final. by the Central Election Commission - CEC, on 07.11.2019[1].

ECAP has once started notifying parties with decisions on their grievances.

The Complaints Panel has decided as follows:

The ECAP received 53 complaints based on them in relation to 52 complaints the panel decided to order the CEC to recount 1472 polling stations. While regarding the complaint lodged by the Initiative - AKR - DP Coalition, it has decided to accept the complaint as grounded and has ordered the CEC to remove from the final election result the votes of the voters outside Kosovo who came from Serbia[2].First from this administrative organ was asked to recount 430 polling stations.

23 complaints were dismissed as untimely and inadmissible[3].

25 complaints were rejected as ungrounded[4].

1 complaint is found to be withdrawn[5].

---

[1] PZAP,http://pzap.rks-gov.net/?p=9752,23.11.2019

[2] PZAP,http://pzap.rks-gov.net/?p=9752,23.11.2019

[3] PZAP,http://pzap.rks-gov.net/?p=9752,23.11.2019

[4] PZAP,http://pzap.rks-gov.net/?p=9752,23.11.2019

[5] PZAP,http://pzap.rks-gov.net/?p=9752,23.11.2019

1. Coalition possibility

The LDK and VV coalition impossible, there are many reasons to fail, first of all the completely different program, the commitments for the state of Kosovo are different, VV failed to recognize the developments in Kosovo, there are also many Kosovar politicians who did not favor this anarchic party.

Coalition	possibilities
VV LDK	Remarks : • Complication until reaching agreement? • Expert of two political party work on the details. • Government should have around 12 Ministries • Governance program will be drafted

The LDK is a right-wing party seeking privatization of publicly owned enterprises while VV wants to hold the post as a public asset. VV wants to establish Commercial Bank with people's money, LDK does not support the concept of a state-owned bank, what is common may be the Economic Development Fund.[6] Protecting workers at work, strengthening the labor inspectorate, fining private companies if they do not respect the employment contract, strengthening public funds, paying regular pension contributions every month. Highly needed health protection for all citizens, the law has long been approved by the Assembly and so far no implementation has taken place in the absence of political knowledge and will. State education reform is also an important topic as VV opposes the private education sector as the dominant area of education in Kosovo and

[6] PZAP,http://pzap.rks-gov.net/?p=9752,23.11.2019

requires it to be reformed just as the Public Universities need to be reformed. The development of vocational schools is important to mention by the two main political parties in the state of Kosovo. These two political parties have completely different programs and commitments, the VV program in Kosovo is explained as impossible for a market economy, the VV reform is completely necessary, this party has no proper political framework, and the VV victory is only minimal. 1%, so this does not give this party convenience but should be completely flexible, remarks in the political vocabulary of this party have the other party LDK which is the second party to vote in Kosovo in the October 6, 2019 elections. The biggest difference between these two political parties is the issue of dialogue with Serbia on normalizing relations, the VV is in no hurry to engage in dialogue, and requires review of all Kosovo-Serbia agreements so far, while the LDK fully recognize the agreements reached so far, although some of them may be revised, the LDK requires the implementation of these agreements, including the agreement on the association of Serb municipalities based on the decision of Constitutional Court- ruling referring to this association, which may not have executive powers this association. VV has an unbalanced political vocabulary for many developments both in the region and in Kosovo, public administration reform is needed and is an EU requirement, VV thinks that DE politicization should take place, but it is not the only deep - politicization problem, the problem remains great employment beyond requirements and needs. U.S. support to Kosovo and Serbia in the Dialogue process requires teamwork: Special Presidential Envoy Grenell and State Department Special Representative Matt Palmer together in Berlin. Both will visit Kosovo. Grenell was very clear should be an final agreement Kosovo-Serbia with 3 or 4 month, VV is very skeptic and asked not to be hurry in this process and not to precise month for achieving agreement. In the public opinion, such a coalition is almost impossible, given the great differences, it is thought that these parties cannot develop the state with these contradictions between them. working alongside a coalition, LDK fears VV may run until term ends. The issue of vetting and enforcement in the judiciary is an issue that is well-settled by both parties, the law on vetting is required, while enforcement must be carried out by an independent body of independent professionals, with EU support and support. The problem is complicated and may be hampered by the justice system. VV has stated that it will not form a coalition with PDK, AAK and NISMA, which are considered corrupt parties by the people, which complicates the agreement for a joint government with these parties. If LDK refuses to join coalition with VV then VV will ask again to go to the new election. VV has also stated that it will not go into coalition with the Serbian list manipulated by Serbia.

VV–decision	VV rules: not possible co-governance in coalition with PDK, AAK, NISMA and Serbian List
	Will be new election if failed coalition with LDK

1.1. Political campaign for 6 October election in Kosovo

Pre-election campaign started a month before the elections day, this campaign is illegal by the law on elections in force, however all private television stations in Kosovo have invited parties to present their program opinions, even though the pre-election campaigns were illegal. They were made but ECAP as a body and CEC did not react in front of the fields, for every night there was also some kind of electronic voting online, every citizen who voted electronically on these televisions means breaking the electoral acts in force. The Election Commission is made up of political parties; therefore it was never dictated to this institution to stop this party pre-election. Independent but the members of this institution are nominated by political leaders. The political parties in Kosovo control and count their votes, this is very problematic for neutral work, the biggest problem is the counting of candidate votes for deputies, in this situation each political party counts the votes of its candidates and in these situations there are always abuses.

Pre-election campaign
Remarks: Campaign is illegal by the law on elections in force

Leaders of the two parties that did best in the weekend Kosovo elections have both signaled their interest in forming a coalition government.

The two former opposition parties that won most votes in Kosovo's recent parliamentary elections have expressed willingness to reach a coalition agreement, four days after the voters elected a new parliament.

After Albin Kurti's Vetevendosje party came first in last Sunday's vote, the Democratic League of Kosovo's candidate for prime minister, Vjosa Osmani, on Wednesday on Facebook called for a coalition agreement between them,but as well this party always have some reasons to live negotiation.

"Finally, citizens not only voted but through their votes, called for changes and the punishment of bad governance, this kind of conclusion come from public opinion" LDK declared . "Citizens also decided for the new government that should be composed of the opposition parties [the LDK and Vetevendosje]," but is really which is going to happened? Cityzen they want to see changes as well International Community.

"To me, there is no other alternative left . An LDK-VV coalition has many challenges ahead of it, but it should have only one interest: that of Kosovo's citizens which wants something to change,"

With all the votes apart from postal ballots counted, the Vetevendosje (Self-Determination) party was in the lead after polling 203,052 votes, or 25.49 per cent of the votes cast. It was just ahead of the LDK, which polled 197,702 votes[7], or 24.82[8] per cent of the votes cast.

Kadri Veseli's former ruling Democratic Party of Kosovo, PDK, came in third place, winning only 169,211[9] votes, or 21.24[10] per cent of the votes cast.

Outgoing Prime Minister Ramush Haradinaj's coalition between his Alliance for the Future of Kosovo, AAK and the Social Democrats came fourth with 92,149 votes, or 11.57 per cent of the votes cast. AAK and PSD was very hoped to have around 18% , this time did not happened

---

[7] CEC,https://www.kqz-ks.org/zgjedhjet-e-pergjithshme/zgjedhjet-per-kuvend-te-kosoves-2019/

[8]CEC, https://www.kqz-ks.org/zgjedhjet-e-pergjithshme/zgjedhjet-per-kuvend-te-kosoves-2019/

[9]CEC, https://www.kqz-ks.org/zgjedhjet-e-pergjithshme/zgjedhjet-per-kuvend-te-kosoves-2019/

[10] CEC ,https://www.kqz-ks.org/zgjedhjet-e-pergjithshme/zgjedhjet-per-kuvend-te-kosoves-2019/

On Tuesday night, Vetevendosje's prime ministerial candidate, Kurti, echoed Vjosa Osmani's words, saying that there was "no other option" to a coalition with the LDK. "We cannot substitute the LDK with the PDK, AAK and NISMA," he said, referring to the other parties.It going to happened how will look such a coalition if we talk about performance.

"I will start negotiations with the LDK based on the election result and finally agree. If we cannot find an agreement, we will go to new elections," Kurti told Pristina-based on KTV with enthusiasm to not forget the wish is something and reality something else .

The final composition of the new parliament remains unclear after a coalition formed between two outgoing deputy prime ministers, Fatmir Limaj and his NISMA party and Behgjet Pacolli of the New Kosovo Alliance, AKR, polled below the threshold of 4 per cent of votes cast, at 4.96 [11]per cent, according to public opinion its good because of destructive role of NISMA in education which was leaded 2017-2019 .

The NISMA-AKR coalition's hopes of passing the threshold now rest on uncounted postal ballots, coming mainly from Kosovo's large diaspora.

1.2. Before election and expected opposition

The opposition had hoped to win an absolute majority in the by-elections, although the former opposition was split, with each of the former opposition parties running alone in the new -elections. The public opinion wanted to be in a pre-election coalition LDK -VV, it did not happen, the main problem was who is going to have the Prime Minister, and the political paths were divided. Citizens' enthusiasm subsided when the two parties decided to run alone, the majority reacted negatively and despaired. LDK and VV in these elections were seen as a new hope for Kosovo to fight organized crime and corruption, enrich politicians illegally.

1.3.Kosovo election: Opposition parties claim win

Ex-Opposition parties have claimed the greatest number of votes in Kosovo's general election.

---

[11] CEC ,https://www.kqz-ks.org/zgjedhjet-e-pergjithshme/zgjedhjet-per-kuvend-te-kosoves-2019/

Centre-left Vetevendosje and centre-right Democratic League (LDK) are each expected to win about 25% of the vote. [12]

The election was called in July when Prime Minister Ramush Haradinaj resigned to face questioning by a war crimes court in The Hague.Nobody believe in Kosovo reasons of PM resignation, Haradinaj was motivated from some people in AAK that is better to resign and maybe could have great result in new election, the reason of resignation was problem of tax for Serbia.

It is the fourth election since Kosovo declared independence from Serbia in 2008.

Serbia does not recognize State of Kosovo and with Russia has blocked it from becoming a member of the UN and other international bodies.

- War crimes claims against PM hang over Kosovo vote
- Kosovo hits Serbia with 100% trade tariffs

In talks before the vote, Vetevendosje and the LDK failed to agree on forming a coalition.

Both parties promise to tackle unemployment and fight crime and corruption.

Vetevendosje's leader Albin Kurti said he would "knock on the LDK door" on Monday to start negotiations.

1.4.Can the biggest parties work together?

There are opinions that these two political party LDK and VV do not have nothing in common, but the general demand of the citizens is that these two parties join the coalition for their own good, although hopes are low to see any change. By and large, most of the programmatic points are at odds with Kosovo's market economy and constitution.

The two parties celebrating the most are very different in character

---

[12] CEC, https://www.kqz-ks.org/zgjedhjet-e-pergjithshme/zgjedhjet-per-kuvend-te-kosoves-2019/

Vetevendosje is an anti-establishment Albanian nationalist movement. Its MPs are notorious for disrupting sessions of the National Assembly by lobbing tear gas[13]. The LDK is Kosovo's oldest party - and hopes to install lawyer Vjosa Osmani as the first female prime minister[14].

The two parties failed to reach a coalition agreement before the election - and may take many weeks or month of negotiations to form a new government the risk is to not happened ever this coalition. And can occur difficult situations or can be more complications in future , or may we have a new election?

Meanwhile, the former leaders of the Kosovo Liberation Army are licking their electoral wounds. Voters held their parties largely responsible for endemic corruption and a lack of development.

Mr Haradinaj's party meanwhile is set to win only 11.5 % of the vote.[15]

The 51-year-old served as commander in the 1998-1999 Kosovo conflict, which eventually led to Kosovo declaring independence in 2008.

Mr Haradinaj stepped down so that he could attend court as an ordinary citizen - but was free to stand for re-election because no indictments have yet been announced.

He denies war crimes and has been tried and acquitted twice before at the UN tribunal[16].

Image copyright EPA Image caption The LDK hopes Vjosa Osmani will become Kosovo's first female prime minister in future/

Last November, he imposed a 100% tariff on imports from Serbia in retaliation for Belgrade blocking Kosovo's membership of international organizations.

---

[13] **De Launey, Balkans Correspondent/BBC, October 2019**

[14] **De Launey, Balkans Correspondent/BBC, October 2019**

[15] CEC,https://www.kqz-ks.org/zgjedhjet-e-pergjithshme/zgjedhjet-per-kuvend-te-kosoves-2019/

[16] **De Launey, Balkans Correspondent/BBC,October2019**

- The town where neighbors won't share a coffee
- Land swap could bridge divide for Serbia and Kosovo

He has ignored pleas from Brussels to revoke the tariffs.

Mr Kurti has said his party will abolish the tariffs but will introduce other retaliatory measures against Serbia.

Meanwhile Serbia's President Aleksandar Vucic says Belgrade will hold talks with the Kosovan government once the tariffs have been removed.

US President Donald Trump appointed the US ambassador to Germany, Richard Grenell, as special envoy for peace negotiations between Kosovo and Serbia. Until now Kosovo was recognize from 116 international stats.

Kosovo is recognized by most of the west state but it needs Belgrade, Russia and China to accept its statehood to get a seat in the United Nations.

1.5. Opposition parties overturn Kosovo politics with election victory/euronews[17]

The opposition leftist Vetevendosje (Self- determination) party looked set to come first in Kosovo's parliamentary poll, but it will have to negotiate a coalition to form a government with other political parties. It will not be easy to find a political partners to start a governance in Kosovo , because the proportional system its make a lot a trouble and reflect very negative concerning to established government in Kosovo[18].The result was very tide between two ex -opposition party in Kosovo. Not much hope about future cooperation of this two political party LDK and VV?

Preliminary results showed it had won 26% of votes with 82% of ballots counted, while another opposition party — the centre-right Democratic League of Kosovo (LDK) — won 25% of votes.

1.6. Supporters celebrated in Pristina on Sunday evening

[17] Euonews: Opposition parties overturn Kosovo politics with election victory,October, 2019

[18] Euonews: Opposition parties overturn Kosovo politics with election victory,October, 2019

The early election happened after Prime Minister Ramush Harra-din-aj resigned ahead of questioning in the Hague by an investigation into war crimes in Serbia two decades ago.

The Democratic Party of Kosovo (PDK) was third with 21% while a list headed by the outgoing prime minister, Ramush Haradinaj, got 11.5% of votes.

It signals a new era for politics in the Balkan nation, whose leadership was previously dominated by figureheads from the country's late-1990s ethnic conflict and war of independence[19].

Kosovars will cast their ballots on Sunday, October 6, to pick a new parliament in snap elections.

Rampant corruption, widespread unemployment and sour relations with neighbouring Serbia are themes dominating the poll — and must be addressed if the country is to make progress toward EU membership[20].

The election was triggered when Prime Minister Ramush Haradinaj resigned after a war crimes court in The Hague summoned him for questioning as a suspect. It concerned his role in the 1998-99 insurgency against Serb forces.

Here's what you need to know about the elections.

1.7.Kosovo and Serbia: still at odds

Predominantly Albanian Kosovo declared its independence in February 2008, when Serbia rejected the declaration as illegal but Europe's major powers and the United States recognized the move.

Where do things stand 20 years since the former Yugoslav territories were at the center of one of Europe's most violent conflicts? In short, Serbia considers Kosovo part of its territory but Kosovo considers itself an independent state.

---

[19] Euonews: Opposition parties overturn Kosovo politics with election victory,October, 2019

[20] Euonews: Opposition parties overturn Kosovo politics with election victory,October, 2019

1.8.A history of tension: Serbia-Kosovo relations explained

Both Serbia and Kosovo aspire to EU membership — Serbia as a candidate country and Kosovo as a potential candidate. The EU insists that Serbia must normalize its relations with Kosovo before joining.

In 2013, Kosovo and Serbia agreed to EU-sponsored talks, but little progress has been made since[21].

"These elections are important because the Belgrade-Pristina dialogue is currently completely at a standstill. A resumption of the dialogue is an essential condition for the normalization of relations," said Alessandro Politi, director of the NATO Defense College Foundation[22].

Pristina imposed a 100% tax on Serbian imports, which it says it will only lift once Belgrade recognizes Kosovo as a sovereign state.

One of the key stumbling blocks is the situation of Kosovo's Serb minority concentrated in the north, which Belgrade struggles control. Even some political parties of serb community are against role of Belgrade in Serbian population in Kosovo

In 2018, the Kosovar and Serbian presidents floated the idea of a "border correction" but the proposal was criticised by the likes of Germany, which fears that any territorial exchange risks sparking instability by calling into question other western Balkan borders.

Naim Rashiti, executive director of the Balkans Policy Research Group told Euronews: "Domestically, the row with Serbia is not seen as a priority as people want employment, education and improve their quality of life[23]"

"In the future, we will keep seeing trade warfare between Kosovo and Serbia," the expert added.

1.9.What are the other key issues concerning voters?

---

[21] Euonews: Opposition parties overturn Kosovo politics with election victory,October, 2019

[22] Alessandro Politi, director of the NATO Defense College Foundation,2019

[23] Euronews, Naim Rashiti, executive director of the Balkans Policy Research Group

With Europe's youngest population (the average age is 29), Kosovo has seen annual economic growth averaging 4% over the past decade, yet more than a third of people are unemployed[24].

Over 200,000 Kosovars have left their country and applied for asylum in the European Union since it declared independence, with Kosovo's population now at 1.8 million[25].

Securing a well-paid job often requires hard cash or political connections — indeed, it is this graft that frustrates a younger generation of Kosovars who are more likely to reject traditional parties.

"Young people born after the war understood the value of the liberation struggle, but the corruption that followed filled the pockets of ex-combatants. They can no longer find a job, can no longer have a visa to be able to emigrate and have insufficient services at home", Politi told Euronews[26].

"An important point for Kosovo will be to comply with EU criteria for the fight against corruption, which are well measurable: without this, young Kosovars will not be able to enjoy the system of facilitated visas to find work in the Schengen area," he added[27].

The lack of basic infrastructure is another issue of concern to voters.

"There are entire regions in which 40% of the population lives without sewage," said ISPI researcher Giorgio Fruscione.

1.10.What's the role of the diaspora?

[24] Euonews: Opposition parties overturn Kosovo politics with election victory,October, 2019

[25] Agency for Statistic in Kosovo, Registration of population in 2011

[26] Euonews: Opposition parties overturn Kosovo politics with election victory,October, 2019

27 Euonews: Opposition parties overturn Kosovo politics with election victory,October, 2019

Kosovo's diaspora is estimated between 700,000 and 800,000 people[28].

While Kosovars living abroad used to play an influential role in the country's politics, their influence appears to be fading.

This time, only 35,000 have registered to vote, Rashiti told Euronews, adding that many were now older, second or third-generation immigrants and were "less and less connected to the daily life of Kosovo society[29]."

1.10.1.Who is in the running?

Dissatisfaction with the results delivered by Haradinaj's three-party governing coalition means more support is likely to go to opposition parties, with the centre-right Democratic League for Kosovo (LDK) and the nationalist, left-leaning Vetevendosje competing for first place.

In the last elections in 2017, three former Kosovo Liberation Army leaders-turned-politicians, Haradinaj, Kadri Veseli and Fatmir Limaj formed the coalition, but this time they are standing separately.[30]

Vjosa Osmani, the LDK's candidate for prime minister, said she believed Kosovars were now ready to be led by a woman for the first time.[31]

Vjosa Osmani, leader of the Democratic League of Kosovo (LDK), speaks at a campaign rally in Suhareka, Kosovo, September 27, 2019. Picture taken September 27, 2019.REUTERS/Laura Hasani

“In more than 90% of cases, it is men who are involved in corruption. A woman sees the state and how to take care of our citizens completely differently,” she told Reuters.

Osmani, along with Vetevendosje's Albin Kurti, is trying to harness anger over corruption to win votes.

---

28 Euonews: Opposition parties overturn Kosovo politics with election victory,October, 2019

29 Naim Rashiti ,Director,Euronews, October 2019

30 Euonews: Opposition parties overturn Kosovo politics with election victory,October, 2019

31 LDK candidate for prime minister on election 2019

Both are against making territorial concessions to Serbia.

1.10.2. What is the predicted result?

Opinion polls at the moment suggest no party will get enough support in Sunday's election to form a government, a result that is predicted to lead to prolonged coalition talks.

"The only coalition I can see forming is between the leftwing nationalists and LDK, if they find a consensus on a name," said Fruscione[32].

"The outcome is hard to predict and will largely depend on turnout," usually in proportional system is more complicated[33].

"Ruling parties are likely to lose against the opposition but we have to see how the coalition will be formed," he added[34].

1.10.3.EU observers in election, 6 October 2019

Well-administered and transparent elections affected by an uneven playing field, and marred by intimidation and lack of competition in the Kosovo Serb areas (Pristina, 8 October 2019)[35].

The Chief Observer, Mrs Viola von Cramon-Taubadel, a Member of the European Parliament, presented today the preliminary findings of the European Union Election Observation Mission (EU EOM) on the 6 October early legislative elections in Kosovo[36].

"These early elections were well-administered and transparent. The campaign was vibrant and competitive allowing contestants to campaign

---

[32] Euronews,Fruscione,10.10.2019

[33] Proportional system, Election Law in Kosovo. http://www.gazetazyrtare.com/e-gov/index.php?option=com_content&task=view&id=157&Itemid=56&lang=en,10.09.2019

[34] Euronews,Fruscione,10.10.2019

[35] EU observers in election, 6 October 2019

[36] EU observers in election, 6 October 2019

freely in most of Kosovo." said Mrs von Cramon at a press conference in Pristina[37].

The election day was orderly, and the EU observers positively assessed voting and counting. The Central Election Commission (CEC) ensured the transparency of the process by promptly publishing online preliminary unofficial results for political entities broken down by polling station. Mrs von Cramon added that "Transparency was a key feature of the CEC's work and it is commendable that despite the short time frame, the CEC has completed all electoral preparations on time[38]."The campaign environment in the Kosovo Serb areas was marred by intimidation, which targeted non-Srpska Lista candidates and supporters. Furthermore, misuse of public resources and a lack of transparency concerning campaign finance resulted in an uneven playing field throughout Kosovo[39].

"Recurring systemic problems with the election process identified also by previous observation missions such as provisions for calling early elections in a short timeframe, an unregulated precampaign period and others, need to be addressed in order to bring the election process in Kosovo fully in line with international standards for democratic elections. Said Mrs von Cramon, who also added that: "A set of recommendations presented together with the mission's Final Report will become truly meaningful only when given serious consideration in the next Assembly, and this should be done as soon as possible[40]."

Andrey Kovatchev, Head of the delegation from the European Parliament said: "We very much welcome the overall effective management of the process[41]. However, the issue of campaign finance is an area of ongoing concern that has been raised by previous observation missions. The regulatory framework does not ensure transparency and integrity and it must be strengthened in order to fight corruption and guarantee a healthy democracy."

On election day, the EU EOM deployed 108 observers from 27 EU Member

[37] EU observers in election, 6 October 2019
[38] EU observers in election, 6 October 2019
[39] EU observers in election, 6 October 2019
[40] EU observers in election, 6 October 2019
[41] EU observers in election, 6 October 2019

States as well as Norway and Switzerland across Kosovo. The EU EOM will remain in Kosovo to follow the process at the Count and Results Centre and the resolution of any complaints and appeals, until the certification of final results[42].

1.10.4. Opposition parties beat ‘war wing’ in Kosovo elections

Opposition parties won the night in Kosovo's election Sunday taking the lead over former guerrillas who have dominated politics for the past decade. [43]

The leftist-nationalist Vetevendosje was in first place with 26 percent of the vote, followed by the centre-right LDK who had 25.2 percent after more than three quarters of the ballots were counted, the electoral commission said[44].But it is not still finale result.

The victory of the two opposition parties was a heavy rebuke to parties led by former guerrillas who battled Serbia in the 1990s, paving the way for Kosovo's independence.

"We did not win. We accept the verdict of the people and the PDK moves to the opposition," said Kadri Veseli, leader of the PDK party that has been in power since 2007 and is linked to President Hashim Thaçi.

With no camp taking an absolute majority, the opposition parties will need to unite to seal the PDK's place in the opposition.

While Vetevendosje and LDK have little overlap ideologically, they have already discussed the possibility of joining forces.

---

[42] EU observers in election, 6 October 2019

[43] EU observers in election, 6 October 2019

[44] France 24, Opposition parties beat ‘war wing’ in Kosovo elections

The party with the most votes will be tasked with forming the new government.

If the trend continues, it could be Vetevendosje's leader Albin Kurti, a 44-year-old who first gained fame as a student activist protesting Serbian repression in the 1990s before the war.

He has since become a strident critic of Kosovo's political elite, and his place at the helm would herald a new era for the young democracy.

Sunday's snap poll was called after ex-prime minister Ramush Haradinaj, a former guerrilla commander, resigned in July to face questioning by a special court in The Hague investigating war crimes from the 1998-99 separatist conflict with Serbia.

His party, which was allied with the PDK in the former government but this time ran alone, had one of the weaker showings with 11.6 percent.

The new leaders will now be under heavy pressure from the West to revive talks with Serbia.

The neighbours have yet to normalise ties two decades after they clashed in war, a lingering source of instability in Europe.

Kosovo, a former Yugoslav province, is recognized by most of the West but it needs Belgrade -- and its allies Russia and China -- to accept its statehood so it can get a seat in the United Nations.

Serbia is also under pressure to make peace with Kosovo in order to move forward with its EU accession process.

Yet their EU-led dialogue has been at a standstill for more than a year, with frequent diplomatic provocations souring efforts to build goodwill.

2.'Let them negotiate'

If the dialogue with Belgrade does resume, one of the most sensitive issues will be settling what powers to grant Serb-majority administrations in Kosovo.

There are approximately 40,000 Serbs living in the north and 80,000 scattered in and around a dozen enclaves in other parts of Kosovo, whose population is mainly ethnic Albanian.

Seats reserved for Serb in Kosovo Assembly
• Serbs have 10 reserved seats in parliament.

The Srpska Lista, which aligns with Belgrade, looked set for a landslide.

Speaking in Belgrade, Serbian President Aleksandar Vucic_said he would be ready to talk to Kurti's party if they are deemed the "legitimate representatives" of Kosovo[45].

2.1. Kosovo Voters Want a New Future, but Old Problems Linger

Ever since Kosovo ended its war with Serbia two decades ago, its dominant political figures have all been men who rose to prominence as fighters and held onto power despite failing to secure a lasting peace and presiding over a floundering economy.[46]

But in parliamentary elections on Sunday, a new generation of politicians offered them a serious challenge for the first time.[47] Opposition parties gained ground and the ruling party appeared to take a solid beating at the polls, according to Kosovo Election Commission projections based on 80 percent of votes counted on Sunday night[48].

---

[45] New York Time, Kosovo Voters Want a New Future, but Old Problems Linger,October,2019

[46] New York Time, Kosovo Voters Want a New Future, but Old Problems Linger,October,2019

[47] New York Time, Kosovo Voters Want a New Future, but Old Problems Linger,October,2019

[48]Kosovo Voters Want a New Future, but Old Problems Linger
New York Times , https://www.nytimes.com/2019/10/06/world/europe/kosovo-election-haradinaj-osmani.html

While the bitter division with Serbia remains — the government in Belgrade refuses to recognize Kosovo as an independent nation — and hope for a rapprochement still far-off, observers hope that the vote might provide an opportunity for the country to shake off the corruption and mismanagement of the postwar years and focus on better governance[49].

At the vanguard of those challenging the entrenched leadership is Vjosa Osmani, 38, who grew up among the rubble-strewn ruins of her country, studied international law in the United States, then was elected to Parliament in 2011.[50]

Her party, the Democratic League, was running closely behind the nationalist Vetevendosje party led by Albin Kurti. The tight race — with no party likely to secure more than 30 percent of the vote — will likely set off a fierce competition for prime minister as coalitions are formed in coming weeks. If Ms. Osmani manages to secure power, she would become the country's first female prime minister. "It's important that Kosovo is represented by leaders who have risen in politics through merit, hard work and a resolve to do better," Ms. Osmani said in an interview on the eve of the election. She said that some politicians of the war generation had "failed Kosovo citizens badly[51]."

While much of Eastern and Central Europe has undergone an economic boom in recent years, Kosovo has lagged far behind. Roughly one in four people in Kosovo are unemployed, wages remain among the lowest in Europe, corruption is rampant and organized crime is endemic.[52]

The early elections were called after Prime Minister Ramush Haradinaj resigned in July, - after being summoned to a court in The Hague for

---

[49] 49Kosovo Voters Want a New Future, but Old Problems Linger
New York Times , https://www.nytimes.com/2019/10/06/world/europe/kosovo-election-haradinaj-osmani.html

[50] Kosovo Voters Want a New Future, but Old Problems Linger
New York Times , https://www.nytimes.com/2019/10/06/world/europe/kosovo-election-haradinaj-osmani.html

51Kosovo Voters Want a New Future, but Old Problems Linger
New York Times , https://www.nytimes.com/2019/10/06/world/europe/kosovo-election-haradinaj-osmani.html

[52] Kosovo Voters Want a New Future, but Old Problems Linger
New York Times , https://www.nytimes.com/2019/10/06/world/europe/kosovo-election-haradinaj-osmani.html

questioning about crimes against ethnic Serbs during and after the 1998-99 war. He served as an officer in the Kosovo Liberation Army at the time[53].

Despite having resigned, Mr. Haradinaj competed in Sunday's election. He seemed to have suffered a sound defeat.

As of Sunday night, Vetevendosje — or Self-Determination in English — was leading with 26 percent of the vote ahead of Ms. Osmani's party, which had 25 percent of votes.

The party of a former Parliament speaker, Kadri Veseli, an ally of Kosovo's president, Hashim Thaci, was third with 21 percent and far ahead of Mr. Thaci's longtime political rival, Mr. Haradinaj, who was a distant fourth with 11.5 percent of the vote[54].

Despite their differences, all the candidates know the public is angry, and all have vowed to root out corruption, to fight organized crime and nepotism and to lower unemployment[55]. They have promised to prioritize issues at home before yielding to pressure from the international community to negotiate with Serbia a final settlement on Kosovo's status. Serbia has so far blocked Kosovo from joining the United Nations and other international bodies, and five European Union states still decline to recognize it.[56] A final settlement might also remove a barrier to Serbia one day becoming a member of the European Union[57].

53Kosovo Voters Want a New Future, but Old Problems Linger
New York Times , https://www.nytimes.com/2019/10/06/world/europe/kosovo-election-haradinaj-osmani.html

[54] Kosovo Voters Want a New Future, but Old Problems Linger
New York Times , https://www.nytimes.com/2019/10/06/world/europe/kosovo-election-haradinaj-osmani.html,6 October,2019

55 Kosovo Voters Want a New Future, but Old Problems Linger
New York Times , https://www.nytimes.com/2019/10/06/world/europe/kosovo-election-haradinaj-osmani.html,6 October,2019

[56] Kosovo Voters Want a New Future, but Old Problems Linger
New York Times , https://www.nytimes.com/2019/10/06/world/europe/kosovo-election-haradinaj-osmani.html

57 57Kosovo Voters Want a New Future, but Old Problems Linger
New York Times , https://www.nytimes.com/2019/10/06/world/europe/kosovo-election-haradinaj-osmani.html, 6 October ,2019

" Again this is an opportunity for the older generation with old problems and old politicians to break the cycle of using Serbia as an excuse for the mistakes of Kosovo's governments. VV has leader in age 45 , but this political party is consist by older people in presidency , the mayor body is leading by two people which was part of PDK.VV has electoral vote from people which are tired with other political party in Kosovo which they lead for 12 year with corruption, nepotism and without development of economy and health protection policy.

2.2.Decision on tariffs and dialogue : The first big test after the elections in Kosovo

Relations between Kosovo and Serbia, as well as Pristina's 100% tariffs on goods from Serbia and Bosnia and Herzegovina, are major campaign themes ahead of the snap parliamentary elections in Kosovo, scheduled for 6 October.

The elections are taking place against the backdrop of international actors, such as Washington and Brussels, becoming increasingly explicit in their messages to Belgrade and Pristina, that the normalisation talks must resume, and that the tariffs should be revoked quickly.

Political analist Kosovo and a member of the Balkans in Europe Policy Advisory Group (BiEPAG), stresses for *European Western Balkans* that the abolishing the tariffs and continuation of the dialogue with Serbia will be the first test of the new government after the elections, adding that such a decision will not be easy, especially since the condition for abolishing the tariffs may be that Serbia stops with the de-recognition campaign of Kosovo's independence and obstruction of Kosovo's membership in international organisations.

However, despite the potential political cost of the decision to revoke tariffs and resume the dialogue, election campaign and statements of the candidates for Prime Minister show that the will to pave the way to the solution exists nonetheless. Some of the political parties have so far proposed the removing the tariff and replacing it with reciprocity.

"*Vetëvendosje!* wants the reciprocity approach in which Kosovo will impose the same sanctions to those Serbia imposes toward Kosovo. Whereas, Democratic Party of Kosovo (PDK) is seemingly divided in this regard."

Democratic League of Kosovo (LDK) seems to have the most flexible approach toward the tariffs because many of the key party members have indicated that they are willing to suspend tariffs and constructively deal with the dialogue even yetis early to conclude.

On the other hand, political analysts emphasizes that some Kosovo's leaders, such as Ramush Haradinaj, promote a very risky agenda. Haradinaj is building his campaign on the "100% state" inspired by the 100% tariffs and against exchanging territories, his government has imposed.

Next Government will address tariffs will surely be ready to deal with this fact.

"Election might affect the dialogue process depending on who will form the government. Yet, what the political scene has learned in the last two years is the need for consensus which goes beyond party lines", political parties after elections will have to work on consensus building new government .

2.3.A lukewarm approach to the EU

Dialogue with Serbia has been one of the main conditions for the progress on EU accession path of both countries and, even though the Committee for Civil Liberties, Justice and Home Affairs of the European Parliament reaffirmed its support for visa-free travel of the citizens of Kosovo last week, the process has been slow at best over the past two years.

Our interlocutors assess that, in spite of this, Kosovo's orientation remains towards the West. According to political analyst , public opinion , all political parties in Kosovo give their full support for the Euro-Atlantic agenda of the country.

"Good example of this support was recorded during the last Assembly's legislature when two of the biggest opposition parties were boycotting the proceedings of the Assembly due to the issues related to the Kosovo-Serbia dialogue, yet would come back and vote for EU related legislation".

However, during the current election campaign, the political parties are more cautious in promising visa liberalization or even setting a date for Kosovo's EU membership, which has been also a feature of the previous campaigns.

“Seemingly, the EU is not on the agenda. With the uncertainty surrounding the visa liberalization process citizen are mostly interested to happened soon , political parties in Kosovo are hesitate to include this issue in their programs” because nobody know is going to happened or not during 2019/20.

This has a lot to do with the lack of EU perspective, the sense of isolation, and the general understanding that the EU will not be politically able to deliver.

“The lack of delivery on the EU side might as well be used by the political elite to shift this attitude and re-define country’s foreign strategic partners” in future .

The times of uncertainty, with the new External Action Service being led by a non-recognizer (Spain’s Josep Borell), have contributed to the overall lukewarm approach of political parties toward EU integration process, with the only positive aspect being the lack of tendency to derail from EU or share negative approach or propaganda toward the Union, she concludes. Political parties they do not want the new negotiator come up from Spain with knowing reason.

2.4. Bullying Among Serbs Sours Kosovo's Democratic Gains

Last weekend's vote in Kosovo was widely seen as a democratic feather in the cap of Europe's newest state. But one stubborn problem for minority Serbs stuck out like a sore thumb.

MITROVICA, Kosovo -- When her father reached for the phone at around 6:45 p.m. on election night, he'd been content to sit out the October 6 voting along with the majority of Kosovo's 1.9 million registered voters. [58]

But within moments of hanging up, he was hurrying for the door, along with his wife, to the polling station in their majority-Serb community south of the Ibar River that remains a powerful symbol of Kosovo's ethnic divisions.

---

[58] CEC, https://www.kqz-ks.org/zgjedhjet-e-pergjithshme/zgjedhjet-per-kuvend-te-kosoves-2019/17.02.2021

They had just 15 minutes before polling stations closed, the caller had told him bluntly, and he had to "do his civic duty."It was further evidence, said his daughter, who asked to remain anonymous, of the kind of pressure that they and other ethnic Serbs face across the country.

The pressure, she said, comes not from the ethnic Albanian majority but from other Serbs.

"He [rushed out to vote] because he works for Serbian institutions and fears jeopardizing his job because he didn't go to the polls," she told RFE/RL's Balkan Service. "My mother did the same."

2.5. Punching Above Its Weight

By hook or crook, the party that has controlled nearly all of the 10 seats in Kosovo's 120-seat parliament reserved for ethnic Serbs following each of the last two elections, Srpska Lista, punched above its weight again last week to take 6.6 percent of the national vote.

The **result** reflects strong turnout among ethnic Serbs, who are most densely concentrated north of the Ibar and are thought to make up some 1-2 percent of the national population.

By virtue of its place within each of Kosovo's last two governing coalitions and open support from the government of neighboring Serbia, which still doesn't recognize Kosovo's independence, Srpska Lista's influence extends well beyond mostly Serb communities.

But its methods have been publicly questioned by rival Serb politicians and by election monitors from the European Union, who warned on October 8 that campaigning had been "marred by intimidation, which targeted non-Srpska Lista candidates and supporters."

The three other ethnic Serb parties in the running -- the Kosovar Serbs Party (0.2 percent), the Freedom coalition (0.12 percent), and the

Independent Liberal Party (0.06 percent) -- failed to reach parliament by wide margins.[59]

"In the Kosovo Serb community, parties seeking to compete with Srpska Lista were unable to mount effective campaigns due in part to intimidation of candidates, their families and voters in general," the EU election-observation mission said in its preliminary statement.

"Srpska Lista-controlled municipalities, as well as the government of Serbia, directed Kosovo Serbs to vote only for Srpska Lista, while their opponents were denounced as anti-Serbian."

It was the bleakest aspect of a vote that was otherwise lauded as a major step forward for a still-partially recognized state and an example for others in the turbulent Balkans and beyond.

As a result, the EU observers said, "the electoral process for Kosovo Serbs fell short of...international standards.

"Rival Serb parties have repeatedly accused Srpska Lista itself of thuggery. Freedom (Sloboda) coalition leader Nenad Rasic, at a debate alongside two other Serb party leaders in Caglavica, alleged Srpska Lista intimidation that included the "interrogation" of the wife of a coalition activist and a warning that she would lose her job.

He told RFE/RL's Balkan Service that the intensifying tactics to boost Srpska Lista's support -- including from Belgrade -- since that party's creation six years ago was an attack on self-determination for Kosovar Serbs.

They have imposed the standard that 'whoever is not with us is against us, and whoever is against us is our enemy,'" Rasic said, calling it "a step further" than past behavior.

Elsewhere, Rasic suggested his own life might be in danger.

---

[59] CEC,https://www.kqz-ks.org/zgjedhjet-e-pergjithshme/zgjedhjet-per-kuvend-te-kosoves-2019/

2.6. Alleged Intimidation

Prosecutors in Kosovo were said to be looking into a number of cases of alleged intimidation. Srpska Lista declined to respond to RFE/RL's Balkan Service questions about such allegations.

In 2018, a prominent entrepreneur and influential political voice for Serb-Kosovar dialogue, Oliver Ivanovic, was shot dead outside his party's offices in the predominantly Serb portion of the northern city of Mitrovica[60].

The killing hasn't been solved, but reports say a senior official within Srpska List is wanted for questioning. Meanwhile Ivanovic's former party, the SDP Citizens Initiative, announced in September that it was teaming up with Srpska Lista for the October 6 elections[61].

Based in Mitrovica, Srpska List was created ahead of national elections in 2014, when it garnered about 38,000 votes. In this month's balloting it received more than 52,000 votes, upward of half of the best estimates of Kosovo's entire ethnic Serb population[62].

Its results are watched eagerly in the Serbian capital, where President Aleskandar Vucic has unapologetically stumped for Srpska Lista.

Speculation that the party somehow takes its marching orders from Belgrade are difficult to prove, but the relationship is clearly close.

The EU observation mission noted that "the government of Serbia and the local authorities in the Serb-majority municipalities strongly directed Kosovo Serbs to vote only for Srpska Lista."

The observers cited reports of Serbian officials being turned away at Kosovo's border during the 10-day campaign ahead of the snap elections.

Isidora Stakic, a researcher at the Belgrade Security Policy Center, told RFE/RL recently that their research from February "shows that Serbs living

---

[60] Balkan Insight,October,2019

[61] Balkan Insight, October,2019

[62] Balkan Insight,October,2019

in northern Kosovo are more afraid of representatives of the Serbian authorities than of Albanians."

The "greatest pressure," she said, is from Srpska Lista and its Serbian government allies.

Serbia's president, Aleskandar Vucic, welcomed the October 6 results by saying Srpska Lista had "won its most convincing victory in its history," according to Balkan Insight, adding, "This is one of my favorite wins because it happened under the most difficult conditions[63]."

Many international observers are keen to see any new government in Pristina beat a speedy path to renewed talks with Serbia over normalizing relations between the two ex-Yugoslav neighbors[64].

Those negotiations have been on hold since Vucic abandoned them after Kosovo announced a 100-percent tariff on Serbian imports in November. Their outcome could clear the way for UN recognition for Kosovo, whose statehood is recognized by more than 110 countries but not by Serbia, Russia, China, or Spain, for instance.[65]

The two leading parties in the October 6 elections -- the pro-Albanian Self-Determination party and the Democratic League -- kicked off talks on a possible coalition on October 10.[66]

The EU election observer's mission urged Kosovo's parliament to give the Serb intimidation and other problems "serious consideration...as soon as possible."

Albin Kurti, the leader of Kosovo's leftist Vetevendosje (Self-Determination) party that won a plurality of votes in parliamentary elections, said that dialogue with Serbia has to include the "recognition of Kosovo's independence." Speaking to RFE/RL on October 10 in Pristina, the country's likely future prime minister also said that unless Serbia faces its past, there would be no peace and reconciliation. PRISTINA -- Kosovo's leftist-

[63] Balkan Insight,October,2019
[64] Balkan Insight,October,2019
[65] Balkan Insight,October,2019
[66] Balkan Insight,October,2019

nationalist Vetevendosje (Self-Determination) party and the center-right Democratic League of Kosovo (LDK) have started coalition talks following this weekend's general elections.

"Without wasting time we have started talks with the common idea of a more efficient government and a stronger state," Vetevendosje leader Albin Kurti said on October 10, adding that the expectations of Kosovo's citizens are "very high."

LDK's prime minister candidate, , said that, during their first meeting, the two parties "showed goodwill to govern together and goodwill to work in the interest of citizens."

LDK candidate for PM said they would wait until the final election results before reaching an agreement.

VV and LDK said the parties discussed reducing the number of ministers and deputy ministers.

According to final preliminary results, Vetevendosje garnered 25.5 percent of the vote in the October 6 snap elections, followed by LDK with 24.8 percent there is not final result.[67]

The former ruling party, the Democratic Party of Kosovo (PDK), which has dominated politics for more than a decade, placed third, while the coalition of outgoing Prime Minister Ramush Haradinaj's Alliance for the Future of Kosovo was fourth.

2.7. Turnout was 44.5 percent[68]

EU observers said the polls were "well-administered and transparent," but

---

[67] CEC, https://www.kqz-ks.org/zgjedhjet-e-pergjithshme/zgjedhjet-per-kuvend-te-kosoves-2019/

[68] CEC, https://www.kqz-ks.org/zgjedhjet-e-pergjithshme/zgjedhjet-per-kuvend-te-kosoves-2019/

pointed out shortcomings including the "intimidation" of ethnic Serbs by the main political force that represents the country's Serb minority[69].

The early elections were triggered by Haradinaj's resignation in July after war crimes prosecutors at The Hague summoned him for questioning over his wartime role as a commander of the Kosovo Liberation Army (UCK)[70].

The election campaign was dominated by issues of corruption, high unemployment, and a possible peace deal with Serbia, which has not recognized from 116 international stats.

Kosovo remains very poor, with unemployment at 25 percent. More than 200,000 Kosovars have left and applied for asylum in the European Union since Pristina declared independence in 2008[71].

2.8.Kosovo Election Winner Not In Hurry To Renew Serbia Talks

The leader of the center-left party that won a plurality of votes in Kosovo's early parliamentary elections on October 6 says he isn't hankering to restart formal talks designed to normalize relations with neighboring Serbia.[72]

In an interview with the Associated Press published on October 8, Vetevendosje party chief Albin Kurti, who is poised to become the next prime minister, said that Pristina-Belgrade negotiations aren't currently at the top of his list of things to do[73]."It cannot be top priority on day one of me as a new prime minister," he said.

His party defeated center-right groupings that were formed by former fighters from the Kosovo Liberation Army who had been in power for more than a decade.

Kosovo declared independence from Serbia in 2008 after a decade of fighting an insurgent war amid a crackdown by former Serbian leader Slobodan Milosevic.

[69] Balkan Insight,October,2019
[70] Balkan Insight,October,2019
[71] Balkan Insight,October,2019
[72] Balkan Insight,October,2019

[73] Kosovo Election 2019, Radio Free Europe, https://www.rferl.org/z/679,10.11.2019

Serbia, China, Russia and five European Union countries don't recognize Kosovo's statehood, although more than 117 countries do.

Dialogue between Serbia and Kosovo started in 2011, but has since stalled. A bone of contention includes a 100 percent tariff on Serbian goods[74].

"Only after the principle of reciprocity has been put in place, [then] we can lift the tariffs," Kurti told AP, referring to 33 deals signed between Kosovo and Serbia[75].

Both the EU's probable future foreign-policy chief, Josep Borrell, and the new U.S. special envoy to Kosovo-Serbia, Richard Grenell, have stated that normalizing relations between the neighboring countries is a priority.[76]

Until tensions defuse and relations stabilize, the EU has said prospects of Kosovo and Serbia joining the 28-member bloc remain dim.[77]

Kurti is scheduled to meet Grenell, currently the U.S. ambassador to Germany, on October 9.[78]

2.9. 'First True Transition': Key Takeaways From Kosovo's Watershed Vote

Kurti, who spent 2 ½ years in a Serbian prison for his pro-independence actions, has already sparked the ire of Belgrade.

When asked about a ethnic-Serbian minister in his future government, a constitutional requirement, Kurti said he preferred "a Serb minister who comes from those Serbs who recognize the independence of Kosovo."

---

[74] Kosovo Election 2019, Radio Free Europe, https://www.rferl.org/z/679,10.11.2019

[75] Kosovo Election 2019, Radio Free Europe, https://www.rferl.org/z/679,10.11.2019

[76] Kosovo Election 2019, Radio Free Europe, https://www.rferl.org/z/679,10.11.2019

[77] Kosovo Election 2019, Radio Free Europe, https://www.rferl.org/z/679,10.11.2019

[78] Kosovo Election 2019, Radio Free Europe, https://www.rferl.org/z/679,10.11.2019

This prompted a furious reaction from Belgrade with Marko Djuric, the Serbian official in charge of Kosovar affairs, accusing Kurti of being an "extremist" who was "stomping" on the democratic rights of Kosovo-Serbs.

Following the elections, Kurti's Vetevendosje party asked the center-right Democratic League of Kosovo (LDK) to form a coalition government.[79]

EU observers say Kosovo's elections were "well-administered and transparent," but pointed out shortcomings including the "intimidation" of ethnic Serbs by the main political force that represents the country's Serb minority -- the Belgrade-backed Serb List party.[80]

It won the 10 seats in Kosovo's 120-seat legislature that are reserved for ethnic Serbs.[81]

European Union observers say Kosovo's parliamentary elections were "well-administered and transparent," but pointed out shortcomings including the "intimidation" of ethnic Serbs by the main party representing the country's Serb minority[82].

According to nearly-final preliminary results, the leftist-nationalist Vetevendosje won the October 6 snap elections, but the party did not garner enough votes to rule on its own and is expected to enter coalition talks with the center-right Democratic League of Kosovo (LDK).

The head of the EU Election Observation Mission, European Parliament member Viola von Cramon-Taubadel, presented the preliminary findings of the mission on October 8, saying the campaign was "vibrant and competitive" while election day was "orderly[83]."

However, the campaign environment in the Kosovo Serb areas was "marred

---

79 Kosovo Election 2019, Radio Free Europe, https://www.rferl.org/z/679,10.11.2019
Kosovo Election 2019, Radio Free Europe, https://www.rferl.org/z/679,10.11.2019
80 Constitution of Republic of Kosovo
81 Kosovo Election 2019, Radio Free Europe, https://www.rferl.org/z/679,10.11.2019
82 Kosovo Election 2019, Radio Free Europe, https://www.rferl.org/z/679,10.11.2019
83 Kosovo Election 2019, Radio Free Europe, https://www.rferl.org/z/679,10.11.2019

by intimidation, which targeted non-Srpska Lista candidates and supporters," a statement said.

"Misuse of public resources and a lack of transparency concerning campaign finance resulted in an uneven playing field throughout Kosovo," it added.

With more than 99 percent of the ballots counted, results from the Central Election Commission showed Vetevendosje garnered 25.5 percent of the vote followed by LDK with 24.8 percent.[84]

The former ruling party, the Democratic Party of Kosovo (PDK), which has dominated politics for more than a decade, placed third with 21.2[85] percent of the vote, while the coalition of outgoing Prime Minister Ramush Haradinaj's Alliance for the Future of Kosovo had 11.5[86] percent.

The turnout was 44 percent, a slight improvement on the previous election two years ago.[87]

Vetevendosje's leader, former student protest leader Albin Kurti, pledged on October 7 to work quickly to try and form a coalition government with LDK, whose prime ministerial candidate is Vjosa Osmani.

3.Urging Reforms

In a joint statement, EU foreign policy chief Federica Mogherini and Enlargement Commissioner Johannes Hahn urged the upcoming government to "swiftly resume work on reforms in support of economic and social development as well as rule of law, on the implementation of the

[84] CEC,https://www.kqz-ks.org/zgjedhjet-e-pergjithshme/zgjedhjet-per-kuvend-te-kosoves-2019/

[85] CEC,https://www.kqz-ks.org/zgjedhjet-e-pergjithshme/zgjedhjet-per-kuvend-te-kosoves-2019/

[86] CEC,https://www.kqz-ks.org/zgjedhjet-e-pergjithshme/zgjedhjet-per-kuvend-te-kosoves-2019/

[87]CEC, https://www.kqz-ks.org/zgjedhjet-e-pergjithshme/zgjedhjet-per-kuvend-te-kosoves-2019/

EU-Kosovo Stabilization and Association Agreement and on the EU-facilitated Dialogue with Belgrade."[88]

Mogherini and Hahn said they "expect all political actors to remain committed to these processes, which are key for Kosovo's future, for progress on its European path, and most importantly for the benefit of the people of Kosovo and of the whole region."[89]

The early election was triggered by Haradinaj's resignation in July after war crimes prosecutors at The Hague summoned him for questioning over his wartime role as a commander of the Kosovo Liberation Army (UCK)[90].

The election campaign was dominated by the issues of corruption, high unemployment, and a possible peace deal with Serbia that would clear the way for Kosovo's membership in the United Nations[91].

Kosovo's independence has been recognized by more than 117 states but not by others, including five EU members, as well as Serbia, Russia, and China.

European Union-sponsored talks aimed at normalizing ties between Pristina and Belgrade stalled last year over Kosovo's decision to impose a 100 percent tax on goods from Serbia.

Kosovo has Europe's youngest population with an average age of 29, and economic growth has averaged 4 percent over the past decade. But it remains very poor -- unemployment is 25 percent -- and more than 200,000 Kosovars have left and applied for asylum in the European Union since Pristina won its independence.[92]

3.1. Kosovo holds election amid calls for resuming Serbia talks...

[88] Kosovo Election 2019, Radio Free Europe, https://www.rferl.org/z/679,10.11.2019
[89] Kosovo Election 2019, Radio Free Europe, https://www.rferl.org/z/679,10.11.2019
[90]Kosovo Election 2019, Radio Free Europe, https://www.rferl.org/z/679,10.11.2019
[91] Kosovo Election 2019, Radio Free Europe, https://www.rferl.org/z/679,10.11.2019
[92] Kosovo holds election amid calls for resuming Serbia talks/Washington Post

Kosovo is holding an early general election Sunday amid calls for leaders to resume dialogue with Serbia over normalizing ties.

The vote comes after the outgoing prime minister resigned following a request from a Hague-based court to question him over crimes against ethnic Serbs during and after the country's 1998-99 war[93].

The election will be Kosovo's seventh since the end of the war, and 1.9 million people are eligible to cast ballots to elect 120 lawmakers.

Kosovo's 2008 independence from Serbia has been recognized by more than 116 countries but not by Belgrade. European Union-sponsored talks aimed at normalizing ties between the two countries stalled last year over Kosovo's decision to impose a 100% tax on goods from Serbia.[94]

Other issues in the election include bringing down the unemployment rate which stands at more than 25%, organized crime and corruption.[95] No single political party is likely to win the vote on its own and coalitions have always proved hard to form and easy to fall apart.

The outgoing prime minister, Ramush Haradinaj, having been questioned in The Hague but not charged, is standing for re-election with his Alliance for Kosovo Future. He faces Vjosa Osmani of the Democratic League of Kosovo, the first-ever female candidate for prime minister in the country; Kadri Veseli of the Democratic Party of Kosovo; and Albin Kurti of the Self-Determination Movement Party, which has used extreme methods like throwing tear gas and water bottles in parliament to protest against deals with Serbia.[96]

All candidates except Osmani are former fighters of the Kosovo Liberation Army, which triggered the 1998-1999 war that ended when NATO intervened on behalf of the Albanian majority[97].

---

[93] Kosovo holds election amid calls for resuming Serbia talks/Washington Post
Kosovo holds election amid calls for resuming Serbia talks/Washington Post
[94] Kosovo holds election amid calls for resuming Serbia talks/Washington Post
[95] Kosovo holds election amid calls for resuming Serbia talks/Washington Post
[96] Kosovo holds election amid calls for resuming Serbia talks/Washington Post
[97] Kosovo holds election amid calls for resuming Serbia talks/Washington Post

Kosovo's relations with Serbia have soured further recently after Haradinaj set a 100% tariff on Serb and Bosnian goods last year as a way to get Serbia to recognize Kosovo and to end efforts to prevent it from participating in international organizations.

All political parties, except for Haradinaj's and one closely allied to him, have criticized the tariff. Fearing a loss of votes, none has explicitly said they would lift or suspend it and resume talks, despite pressure from the U.S. and EU.

Instead, Osmani and Kurti say the tariff should be replaced with reciprocity in the application of 33 agreements signed with Belgrade since 2011.

"That was a perfectly legitimate measure although it was done for the wrong reasons," LDK said.

"The majority of political parties are clear in their stance to continue the dialogue, to stick to the international partners' requests," says Evliana Berani, editor-in-chief of Infoglob, an independent online media page. "I am sure each party will start from the beginning to deal with the tax[98]."

Though there are no reliable polls before voting, it is believed by political observers that the opposition may have the upper hand because Osmani and Kurti haven't been embroiled in widespread corruption scandals.[99]

Trade, retail and construction are the main sectors of the economy and the industrial sector is weak. The country also has a strong dependence on remittances from the diaspora, mainly in Germany and Switzerland, which has reached up to 14% of gross domestic product.[100]

"Kosovo is at a crossroads, with high level of unemployment and poverty, with high level of migration and a pessimistic sentiment of the people," says Berani, convinced that whoever wins the election "will be forced to change drastically the way Kosovo is governed. People are tired of 'major' ideas."

---

[98] Evliana Berani, editor in-chief of Infoglob

[99] IPKZH,Curuption in Kosovo,12.02.2021

[100] Kosovo holds election amid calls for resuming Serbia talks/Washington Post

The Serb minority, with 10 seats in the 120-seat parliament, remains a key player in Kosovo, especially since their votes may be needed in a coalition to form a Cabinet, a scenario that occurred two years ago.

The Belgrade-backed Srpska Lista, or Serb List, group is expected to garner the most votes in the Serb-run part of the country amid a fierce campaign that calls for Serb unity. Ten other seats belong to different minorities.

The European Union has sent a 61-member team of observers for the election to show that Pristina "remains a political priority."

3.2. West tells Kosovo and Serbia to return to negotiating table

Four European countries and the United States urged Kosovo and Serbia on Tuesday to re-launch their dialogue on normalizing ties in order to advance their bid for EU membership. [101]

The EU-sponsored dialogues between Belgrade and Pristina was halted last November when Kosovo introduced a 100 percent tax on goods produced in Serbia, pledging to remove it only when Belgrade recognizes Kosovo as a sovereign state. [102]

"The status quo prevents progress on Kosovo's and Serbia's path toward the European Union (EU) and is simply not sustainable," said the so-called Quint group of the United States, Italy, France, Germany and Britain.

They urged both parties to remove obstacles for a dialogue first.

"For Kosovo, that means suspending the tariffs imposed on Serbia. For Serbia, that means suspending the de-recognition campaign against Kosovo," a joint statement said. [103]

Kosovo, with a 90 percent ethnic Albanian majority, declared independence from Serbia in 2008, nearly 10 years after NATO bombing drove Serb forces out of the country. It has been recognized by 117 states but not by five EU member states, Serbia and Russia.

---

[101] Kosovo holds election amid calls for resuming Serbia talks/Washington Post

[102] Kosovo holds election amid calls for resuming Serbia talks/Washington Post

[103] Kosovo holds election amid calls for resuming Serbia talks/Washington Post

Serbia still considers Kosovo part of its territory and has blocked Pristina's membership in international organizations including Interpol and UNESCO. It has also asked some countries to revert their decision to recognize Kosovo as a sovereign state. Marko Djuric who is the head of the Serbian government's Office for Kosovo said the five countries that wrote the letter were in favor of unconditional recognition of Kosovo.

He said that Serbia had acknowledged the letter but that "the policy toward Kosovo will be guided by interests".

Pristina's new official negotiating team for talks with Belgrade in Brussels has agreed what it calls a 'Dialogue Platform' for negotiations on a final and legally-binding agreement on the normalization of relations with Serbia – including a demand that Belgrade pledges to recognize Kosovo.[104]

The negotiating platform, which BIRN has seen, was delivered to parliament speaker Kadri Veseli on Friday and will soon be put to a vote in the legislature.

The first principle agreed by the negotiators says that Kosovo's main goal is to obtain recognition from Serbia with four legally binding promises, including the dropping of Belgrade's objections to Kosovo joining the UN.[105]

The platform document says that Pristina wants "the halting of all activities that hinder Kosovo on the journey towards its international recognition as an independent and sovereign country; the respecting of the territorial sovereignty and integrity of the Republic of Kosovo; the halting of objections, or the encouraging of third parties to object to, the application of the Republic of Kosovo to join international organizations, including the UN, the Council of Europe, the OSCE, and their agencies; and giving up all forms of interference in the internal matters or international relations of the Republic of Kosovo".[106]

The platform insists that a final deal with Belgrade must include an agreement to establish a new tribunal "for the investigation, prosecution

[104] Kosovo holds election amid calls for resuming Serbia talks/Washington Post
[105] Kosovo holds election amid calls for resuming Serbia talks/Washington Post
[106] Kosovo holds election amid calls for resuming Serbia talks/Washington Post

and adjudication of war crimes committed by Serbia in Kosovo in 1998 and 1999".[107]

The suggestion of a new court to try Serbs comes as the Kosovo Specialist Chambers, a Hague-based tribunal set up to try former Kosovo Liberation Army guerrillas and others for wartime crimes in Kosovo, prepares to issue its first indictments.

The Kosovo negotiators' platform also says that issues like wartime missing persons, victims of wartime sexual violence and reparations for war damage should become part of the negotiations with Serbia.

The platform includes a further principle which states that the territory of Kosovo shall not be altered.

Kosovo's President Hashim Thaci caused controversy last year when he suggested that there might be a "border correction" with Serbia as part of a final deal to normalise relations.

The issue caused a serious rift between Thaci and Prime Minister Ramush Haradinaj, who strongly opposes any border changes such as an exchange of territory with Serbia.

After delivering the platform to the parliament speaker, the joint leader of the negotiation team, Fatmir Limaj, urged MPs to adopt it.

"The principles are ones that guarantee peace in this part of the region. Everyone should get it clear that Kosovo is going to Brussels for recognition, nothing else," Limaj told media.[108]

According to the platform, the final agreement between Pristina and Belgrade will enter into force only after "a) Serbia has recognised Kosovo, b) a referendum for the agreement has been held in Kosovo, and c) the agreement is ratified by the parliaments of the two countries".[109]

Serbia has vowed never to recognize its former province as independent.

---

[107] Kosovo holds election amid calls for resuming Serbia talks/Washington Post
[108] Kosovo holds election amid calls for resuming Serbia talks/Washington Post
[109] Kosovo holds election amid calls for resuming Serbia talks/Washington Post

Talks between officials from Pristina and Belgrade have been ongoing in Brussels since 2013, and a successful outcome is seen as crucial to both countries' hopes of joining the EU.[110]

However the talks are currently suspended amid a row over Kosovo's imposition of import taxes on Serbian goods.

3.3.Austria's Petritsch 'Not Against' Kosovo-Serbia Border Changes

Austrian diplomat Wolfgang Petritsch on Thursday said he would not oppose Kosovo and Serbia changing their borders – if this formed part of a mutually agreed, non-violent comprehensive settlement. Veteran Austrian diplomat Wolfgang Petritsch on Thursday said that while he generally opposed territorial changes in principle – in the case of a mutual agreement between Kosovo and Serbia, he would not reject the idea.[111]

"I'm one of the few who, when this idea appeared ... did not belong to these people who automatically said 'No'," he told BIRN Kosovo's TV show *Jeta ne Kosove*.

"I believe this is the first time that I can think of where, in terms of a change of borders, the two sides have decided to look into this issue together," Petritsch told the show.

Petritsch has years of direct experience in the Balkans, having served as the international community's High Representative to Bosnia and Herzegovina.

He was later Austria's Representative to the UN in Geneva, and later on its Representative to the OECD in Paris. He now chairs Austria's Marshall Plan Foundation.

He added that while in Balkan history border corrections were always bloody and one-sided arrangements – if Kosovo and Serbia agreed to such changes in a non-violent, negotiated way, as part of a compromise, it would not be excluded under OSCE rules.

---

[110] Kosovo holds election amid calls for resuming Serbia talks/Washington Post
[111] Kosovo holds election amid calls for resuming Serbia talks/Washington Post

When asked how a state like Serbia can negotiate about territory with a country it does not recognise, Petritsch stated that the agreement would have to involve Serbia's full international recognition of Kosovo.

"If you want to change borders, you first have to recognise the country with whom you want to change borders," he said.

"And this is why I am not for the exchange of territories, but I am not against it," he said, adding that "this idea has been on the Brussels table for more than a year".

Petritsch said the only way to get Russia to abstain from using its veto on the UN Security Council, to stop Kosovo from entering the United Nations, is via Belgrade, with a final result agreed between the two countries.[112]

Petritsch sees that window of opportunity closing soon, however, as he said the elections in the European Union next May will see pro-Russian right-wing nationalists making big advances.

"The next EU elections are going to be a huge advance, if not a victory, for the right-wing populists," he said, going on to name Hungarian Prime Minister Viktor Orban, Poland's Jaroslaw Kaczynski, and Italy's Matteo Salvini, as likely beneficiaries.[113]

"They are best friends with [Russian President Vadimir] Putin. They are going to have their commissioners sitting in the EU Commission. These governments are not going to support Kosovo," Petritsch pointed out.[114]

As for the five EU countries that have not recognized Kosovo's independence – Slovakia, Spain, Romania, Greece and Cyprus – Petritsch said that he had spoken with representatives of each of them, and, if the two sides agreed on a solution, those five EU countries "will definitely agree to it".

---

[112] Kosovo holds election amid calls for resuming Serbia talks/Washington Post
[113] Kosovo holds election amid calls for resuming Serbia talks/Washington Post
[114] Kosovo holds election amid calls for resuming Serbia talks/Washington Post

Spain's Catalan problem, according to Petritsch, would not affect matters, as the two situations were not similar; "no mutual agreement between Barcelona and Madrid exists".

In the case of Kosovo and Serbia, on the other hand, "the two sides want to hammer out a compromise".[115]

Earlier this week, Austria's conservative Chancellor, Sebastian Kurz, said Vienna would not oppose any eventual agreement between Kosovo and Serbia, even if it included changing the borders.

3.4. Austria 'Will Not Oppose' Kosovo-Serbia Border Changes

Ex Austrian Chancellor Sebastian Kurz said that Vienna will not oppose any eventual agreement between Kosovo and Serbia, even if it includes the changing of the borders between the two countries. Austrian Chancellor Sebastian Kurz said on Tuesday during an official visit to Kosovo that Vienna will support any agreement that is reached between Pristina and Belgrade, even if it includes what Kosovo President Hashim Thaci has described as a 'border correction'.

"I have a clear stance – the federal government of Austria agrees with any agreement reached between Kosovo and Serbia. Nobody will be against that agreement," Kurz said during a joint press conference with Thaci.

"This is within the EU, whatever the agreement is, even if it is a border correction or something else, the agreement reached will have our support," Kurz added.

Kurz made a similar statement during his visit to Belgrade a day before travelling to Pristina.

"If there is an agreement that can bring peace, we will not impede that agreement, we will support it," he told media in the Serbian capital on Monday.

---

[115] Kosovo holds election amid calls for resuming Serbia talks/Washington Post

Last month, Thaci stated that a proposal for ethnic Albanian-populated regions of southern Serbia to join Kosovo would be one of the topics discussed at EU-mediated negotiations with Serbian President Aleksandar Vucic.

After Thaci's suggestion that there could be a "border correction", Kosovo opposition parties proposed a resolution saying that no one has a mandate to negotiate over Kosovo's territory, but it could not attract enough votes to pass in parliament last week.

The idea has caused a serious clash between Thaci and Kosovo's Prime Minister Ramush Haradinaj.

During a press conference with Haradinaj directly after the one with Thaci, Chancellor Kurz did not mention the 'border correction' issue.

3.5.Kosovo President Claims Macron Supports Border Correction

President Hashim Thaci of Kosovo claims French President Emmanuel Macron supports his controversial proposal for a border 'correction' with Serbia – despite strong opposition to the idea at home. Kosovo President Hashim Thaci told the public broadcaster of Albania, TVSH, on Thursday that the French President, Emmanuel Macron, supports his idea about a border "correction" with Serbia that might enable ethnic Albanians living in southern Serbia to join Kosovo.

Thaci has been meeting the French leader at the summit of francophone nations taking place in Armenia.

"President Macron strongly supports the Kosovo–Serbia dialogue, the possibility of reaching an agreement within a short period of time, and the real possibility of border correction, which implies Presevo, Medvedja and Bujanovac joining Kosovo," Thaci told TVSH.

Thaci stated that this would pave the way to Kosovo's Euro-Atlantic integration – adding that the border would not be corrected along ethnic lines and would safeguard Kosovo's multi-ethnicity.

"President Macron strongly supports dialogue and a possible border correction," Thaci was quoted as saying. He has stated before that he will bring the idea of a border correction with Serbia to the negotiating table in Brussels as part of a potential final deal with Belgrade, despite strong opposition at home to any territorial exchanges.

The idea has caused a serious clash between President Thaci and the Prime Minister of Kosovo, Ramush Haradinaj.

After Haradinaj declared the idea "dead" on Monday, Thaci called on him to "correct" his statements, calling him "unserious and irresponsible".

"The interesting statement made by the PM shows that he is either in a good mood or feels comfortable in his post," Thaci said.

Serbia's Prime Minister, Ana Brnabic, reacted to Thaci's statement on Friday, saying that Kosovo's government should stop talking about Presevo, Bujanovac and Medvedja and asked Pristina "not to [discuss] further the territory of central Serbia".

She also stressed that Serbia and Kosovo should talk about whether they can reach a compromise that would ensure a long-term normalisation of Belgrade-Pristina relations.

The French government has yet to confirm Thaci's claim.

Europe and the US have sent mixed signals about the proposal, with Germany's Angela Merkel calling border changes in Europe unacceptable. Washington's response has been more nuanced.

Many experts have condemned the idea of border changes as likely to open up a host of other territorial disputes in Europe.

This article has been updated on October 12, 2018, to add Serbian PM Ana Brnabic's statements.

3.6.Opposition Demands Vote to 'Protect Kosovo's Territory'

Kosovo's opposition parties are demanding an extraordinary parliamentary session to put a resolution aimed at protecting the country's territorial integrity against possible border changes with Serbia to a vote. Kosovo opposition parties have called for an extraordinary parliamentary session on

September 4 to put a resolution to a vote which they say will protect the country's territorial integrity amid controversial suggestions of a land swap with Serbia as part of a final deal between Pristina and Belgrade.

The resolution will confirm that "nobody has the mandate to negotiate on Kosovo's territory", Avdullah Hoti, the chief of the opposition Democratic League of Kosovo, LDK's parliamentary group, wrote on Facebook on Monday.

Hoti also said on Tuesday he welcomed the support for the initiative from two other opposition parties, Vetevendosje (Self-Determination) and the Social Democratic Party, PSD.

In order to call an extraordinary parliamentary session, 40 MPs' signatures are required.

"Signatures are being collected, the resolution is already drafted, but there are some details being fixed," the chief of the PSD's parliamentary group, Dardan Sejdiu, told BIRN on Tuesday.

The initiative by the Kosovo opposition comes after an announcement that the presidents of Kosovo and Serbia, Hashim Thaci and Aleksandar Vucic, will have a meeting on September 7.

The opposition is worried by recent statements by Thaci about a "border correction" with Serbia, which some have interpreted as meaning a land swap.

However Rexhep Selimi, a MP from Vetevendosje, told BIRN that his signature has not been yet requested.

"I am not in Kosovo, but nobody has contacted me yet about the signature [to call an extraordinary session]," Selimi said.

Prime Minister Ramush Haradinaj expressed support for an extraordinary session.

"If there is only one point in this resolution, to not change the territorial borders, it has my vote today, tomorrow and at any time," Haradinaj told a press conference on Tuesday.

A Pristina-based watchdog body, the Kosovo Democratic Institute, KDI, also said on Tuesday that it supported the opposition initiative.

“The Republic of Kosovo has entered the final phase of the dialogue without a state strategy approved in its Assembly, without defining the topics of discussion, red lines, deadlines, Kosovo party expectations in this process, and without legitimising Kosovo’s leading team in these talks through a resolution”.

Meanwhile Vetevendosje has not ruled out the possibility of organizing protests against the Thaci-Vucic meeting.

“Society will have full democratic legitimacy in showing Hashim Thaci his place through massive protests,” the chief of Vetevendosje’s parliamentary group, Glauk Konjufca, told Kosovo’s KTV on Monday evening.

But the speaker of parliament Kadri Veseli, who is the head of the ruling Democratic Party of Kosovo, PDK, said that the initiative for calling the extraordinary session “represents politically an absurd and totally unnecessary act about a topic which it has been said will be discussed”.

Veseli wrote on Facebook that the opposition “panic” is dangerous for the country’s stability.

“They have one purpose only, which is to provoke tension followed by violent, anti-democratic protests against the constitutional and legal order in the country,” Veseli said.

But the leader of the PSD, Shpend Ahmeti, wrote on Facebook that it is Veseli’s legal duty to call the session.

Ahmeti said it was important when Thaci was apparently intending to discuss “‘correcting the border’ with a country which does not recognize the sovereignty and territorial integrity of our country”.[116]

4.Serbia, Kosovo Presidents Vow For New Historic Deal

---

[116] Blerim Burjani, IKPZH,Dialog Kosovo-Serbia, 2018,p67,Pristina

Serbia's and Kosovo's presidents have called on the international community to support the deal reached by the two countries, including possible border corrections. Serbian President Aleksandar Vucic and his Kosovo counterpart, Hashim Thaci, said on Saturday evening that it's time to make new history with a deal between Kosovo and Serbia, underlining the importance of EU integrations for both countries.[117]

"It is time for us to make new history," Kosovo President Thaci said on Saturday evening, speaking on a panel with Vucic at the European Alpbach political forum in Austria.

The event, called "New perspectives on EU enlargement", comes ahead of Thaci and Vucic's next meeting in Brussels on September 7 for the new round of EU-facilitated dialogue aimed to resolve the decades-long dispute between the two countries.[118]

"Nobody needs to be afraid or concerned about negotiations," Thaci said, and added that the only way forward for both Kosovo and Serbia is EU integration.

"The time for an agreement between Kosovo and Serbia is now. And we have a short window of opportunities," he said.

Meanwhile, Vucic called on the international community to allow Serbs and Albanians to resolve the Kosovo issue on their own and expressed dissatisfaction over the desire of other countries to influence the content of a possible agreement between Belgrade and Pristina, Beta news agency reported.

"Now we are trying to do something that is of great importance to our future, something that is very important for the Albanians also. We must live together, we are the two most numerous people in the Balkans. If we cannot solve it, who will?" Vucic was qouted saying.

"I am just an ordinary man trying to influence in a way that I can keep peace and tranquility," Vucic said.

---

[117]Blerim Burjani, IKPZH,Dialog Kosovo-Serbia, 2018,p.56 ,Pristina
[118] Blerim Burjani, IKPZH,Dialog Kosovo-Serbia, 2018,p.46,Pristina

"We have just witnessed a very historic moment," EU Enlargement Commissioner Joannnes Hahn said after Thaci and Vucic had spoken.

He also expressed his belief that it's up to Vucic and Thaci to build a solution, following what US President Donald Trump's national security advisor, John Bolton, said in Kiev on August 24: that the US will not exclude or oppose territorial swaps between Serbia and Kosovo if the two sides can agree on them.

"Whatever the solution is, and we should not exclude anything, should contribute to stability in the region and this solution should not trigger any ideas... [I] need to assure the international community that this is a tailor-made solution contributing to the overall goal contributing to peace," Hahn said.

"We will not impose something from outside. But again, any solution must be tailor-made to contribute to regional stability, not trigger instability somewhere else. We need this reassurance," Hahn added.

On Saturday, the EU's foreign policy chief, Federica Mogherini, announced that Vucic and Thaci will meet on September 7 in Brussels.

"The High Representative will continue the discussions with the two Presidents on the comprehensive normalization agreement with a view to making concrete progress, given the priority attached to the EU-facilitated dialogue between Belgrade and Pristina and the European Union perspective of the region," the press release said.

Serbian President Vucic also announced last week that he will visit Kosovo on September 9 to present the "guidelines and directions of state policy towards Kosovo".

Kosovo declared independence from Serbia in 2008, which Belgrade opposes. However, the EU's main precondition for Serbia's bid for EU membership is for it to normalise relations with Kosovo.

Serbia's leadership, including President Aleksandar Vucic, is thought to be pushing for a territorial swap as a way to finally resolve the dispute and so move on with Serbia's EU membership aspiration.

However, this idea has met with disproval from the Serbian opposition, many Kosovo Serbs, and from German Chancellor Angela Merkel as well.

On the other side, Kosovo President Thaci said on August 8 that a deal might be reached with Belgrade for the predominantly Albanian municipalities of southern Serbia – Presevo, Medvegja and Bujanovac – to become part of Kosovo.

4.1.US Won't Oppose Serbia-Kosovo Border Changes – ex advisore – Bolton

President Donald Trump's national security advisor, John Bolton, said in Kiev that the US will not exclude or oppose territorial swaps between Serbia and Kosovo if the two sides can agree on them. US President Donald Trump's National Security Advisor, John Bolton, said on Friday that Washington will not weigh in on the controversial idea of a territorial swap between Serbia and Yugoslav former province of Kosovo.

"The US policy is that if the two parties can work it out between themselves and reach agreement, we don't exclude territorial adjustments," he said in Kiev, Ukraine, on Friday.

"We would not stand in the way, and I don't think anybody in Europe would stand in the way if the two parties to the dispute reached a mutually satisfactory settlement," Bolton added.

Bolton is the highest ranked US official to address the topic of partition, which gained momentum after the US ambassador to Kosovo, Greg Delawie, showed reluctance to definitively say whether a territory swap was 54 acceptable to Washington.

Bolton spoke out against Kosovo's 2008 unilateral declaration of independence long before he became Trump's National Security Advisor.

The US and most EU countries acknowledge Kosovo's independence within its existing borders. However, Serbia does not – and maintains control over the mostly-Serb populated far north of the country.

Serbia's leadership, including President Aleksandar Vucic, is thought to be pushing for a territorial swap as a way to finally resolve the dispute and so move on with Serbia's EU membership aspiration. But the idea has met with disproval from the Serbian opposition, many Kosovo Serbs, and from German Chancellor Angela Merkel as well. As debate about the potential partition of Kosovo heats up and Belgrade-Pristina negotiations seem to be entering their final stage, BIRN asked seven experts to suggest solutions to the dispute and assess the possible consequences of territorial exchange.

Since June, both sides in the EU-mediated talks on the normalisation of relations between Serbia and Kosovo have stated that the negotiations are entering their final stage.

At the same time, there has been increasingly heated talk of an exchange of territories – swapping Albanian-majority areas in southern Serbia for Serb-majority ones in northern Kosovo – although this has never been an official topic of discussion during the Belgrade-Pristina dialogue in Brussels.

BIRN asked seven experts to give their opinions about what kind of final deal could be achieved between Belgrade and Pristina, and what the partition of Kosovo and an exchange of territories could lead to in practice.

4.2.'Both sides are interested in a cold peace'

Florian Bieber, professor for Southeast European History and Politics at the University of Graz and Coordinator of the Balkans in Europe Policy Advisory Group:

- Potential solution to the Serbia-Kosovo dispute

"While the partition idea keeps resurfacing, the EU and key members have stated their red lines against partition.

"There are numerous reasons why such a solution would lead nowhere or rather risk further tensions and conflict. The realistic solution would have to ensure that Kosovo's independence becomes accepted, especially in the UN and by the five EU non-recognisers.[119]

[119] Florian Bieber, professor for Southeast European History and Politics at the University of Graz and Coordinator of the Balkans in Europe Policy Advisory Group:

"Whether Serbia formally recognises Kosovo or finds another way is flexible, but it has to be clear that Serbia de facto recognises Kosovo.

- Kosovo's partition and an exchange of territories

"I seriously doubt that an agreement would end the tensions and the dispute. Both sides are interested in a cold peace, not a new page in their relationship.[120]

"Both keep presenting the dispute as a zero-sum game and unlike the Macedonian and Greek governments, don't seem ready to form a partnership to transform the conflict. They are both seeking to benefit from tensions in the future. After all, the conflict is a useful distraction both for the domestic audience and towards the EU.[121]

"Once the Kosovo-Serbia dispute is settled, Serbian President Vucic would be confronted with more critical voices from the EU about the state of democracy and rule of law, thus he has a strong incentive not to find a settlement soon, and in Kosovo, the government suffers from a fragile coalition with a weak legitimacy, also making it unlikely to make any compromises.[122]

"Considering the scepticism of EU members also raises the question what the EU can offer for a settlement. France and the Netherlands will remain deeply skeptical about enlargement, even if both settle.[123]

"Thus, the decision on Macedonia and Albania acted as a disincentive for a compromise, as both governments ask, what can we get from the EU if we compromise?, and the answer from the EU is not clear."

4.3.'Some form of compromise'[124]

---

[120] Florian Bieber, professor for Southeast European History and Politics at the University of Graz and Coordinator of the Balkans in Europe Policy Advisory Group:

[121] Florian Bieber, professor for Southeast European History and Politics at the University of Graz and Coordinator of the Balkans in Europe Policy Advisory Group:

[122] Florian Bieber, professor for Southeast European History and Politics at the University of Graz and Coordinator of the Balkans in Europe Policy Advisory Group:

[123] Florian Bieber, professor for Southeast European History and Politics at the University of Graz and Coordinator of the Balkans in Europe Policy Advisory Group:

Edward Joseph, Adjunct Professor and Senior Fellow, Johns Hopkins School of Advanced International Studies:

- Potential solution to the Serbia-Kosovo dispute

"Resolution of the nearly intractable Balkan disputes rests on one factor above all: Western political will. So, 'the solution' for Kosovo doesn't happen in a vacuum; it reflects the continuum of political will not just in Europe but in Washington as well.[125]

"As for what [Serbian President Aleksandar] Vucic can accept on Kosovo, as long as 'the solution' concretely and directly advances Belgrade's EU accession, he can – and will – accept almost anything that protects the position of Serbs in Kosovo.[126]

"The whole notion that Vucic faces some 'choice' between the EU or Russia is a distortion promoted by Vucic himself to dampen Western pressure.[127]

"It is entirely possible that 'the solution' on Kosovo would entail quasi-recognition by Belgrade in exchange for asymmetrical protections for Serbs in the north and south of Kosovo — provided the EU demands it and is prepared to move forward on enlargement."

- Kosovo's partition and an exchange of territories

"Territorial division is the bane of the Balkans. The notion that borders are malleable – that RS[Bosnia's Serb-dominated entity Republika Srpska] could secede from Bosnia, for example, or that Croats could get their own entity

---

[124] Edward Joseph, Adjunct Professor and Senior Fellow, Johns Hopkins School of Advanced International Studies:

[125] Edward Joseph, Adjunct Professor and Senior Fellow, Johns Hopkins School of Advanced International Studies:

[126] Edward Joseph, Adjunct Professor and Senior Fellow, Johns Hopkins School of Advanced International Studies:

[127] Edward Joseph, Adjunct Professor and Senior Fellow, Johns Hopkins School of Advanced International Studies:

[in Bosnia and Herzegovina], itself a precursor to eventual secession – is what helps entrench Bosnia's political polarisation.[128]

"The same mentality is what promotes Serb intransigence in the north of Kosovo; why compromise and cooperate with Pristina as Serbs in the south do, when – if you only hold out – you might be able to secede from Kosovo altogether?[129]

"Fortunately, the breakthrough agreement between Greece and Macedonia on the latter's name will – if the agreement survives – put a damper on division. If the name agreement enters into force, division of Macedonia is taken off the table and the country heads to NATO membership, virtually guaranteeing that the country will not be divided, no matter how restive Albanians become.[130]

"And that automatically complicates division of Kosovo, because it makes it harder to 'compensate' Albanians there for the loss of the north. Of course, the converse is true; if there is no agreement on the name, and a movement for division of Kosovo gains momentum, then you can count on calls to hive off Albanian majority areas of Macedonia, a messy and dangerous step that only invites and incites more claims on the country.[131]

"Those who think that Presevo Valley/South Serbia represents the 'swap' solution for the north have not spoken to the Albanians who live there. Many Albanians who live in Presevo do not relish the idea of becoming an eastern province of Pristina, cut off from the vital north-south highway that Serbia will not relinquish.[132]

"The idea that Kosovo should be divided rests on illusions — that it would be 'just', that it would be feasible and containable rather than messy, impractical and dangerous. The more it's talked about, the more it will

---

[128] Edward Joseph, Adjunct Professor and Senior Fellow, Johns Hopkins School of Advanced International Studies*:*

[129] Edward Joseph, Adjunct Professor and Senior Fellow, Johns Hopkins School of Advanced International Studies*:*

[130] Edward Joseph, Adjunct Professor and Senior Fellow, Johns Hopkins School of Advanced International Studies*:*

[131] Edward Joseph, Adjunct Professor and Senior Fellow, Johns Hopkins School of Advanced International Studies*:*

[132] Bodo Weber, Senior Associate of the Democratization Policy Council,12.01.2021

appear as a practical solution – which it isn't. The fact that the EU has extraordinary leverage is what makes the whole subject of territorial division of Kosovo not just impractical and dangerous, but unnecessary."

4.4.'Explicit or implicit recognition of Kosovo'

[133]Bodo Weber, Senior Associate of the Democratization Policy Council:

- Potential solution to the Serbia-Kosovo dispute

"Negotiations are indeed entering into the final stage, that is over a final, comprehensive and legally binding agreement on full normalisation – as both parties, particularly Belgrade, did not make use of the gradual, less painful approach the original political dialogue initiated in 2012-13 offered.[134]

"The final solution, at least of the status issue, is clear by 'the original dialogue deal', its framework and ultimate aims as more or less explicitly defined in 2011-13, and accepted by both parties, including Belgrade.[135]

"That is a solution based on the reality that Serbia lost Kosovo, primarily due to its own policy of the last three decades. It means territorial integrity and sovereignty of Kosovo, full exercise of international subjectivity, including an EU membership perspective and Serbian support for a UN seat.

"Recognition of Kosovo as an independent state by Serbia, whereby if Serbia insists this to happen in a reduced and not full formal legal form, it has to explain and guarantee how all the aims of the final agreement can be secured this way, too.

"Finally, forms of ethnic representation and positive discrimination as embodied in the Association of Serb Majority Municipalities need to guarantee the institutional functionality of the state of Kosovo and have safeguards against any future secession of Kosovo north.

[133] Bodo Weber, Senior Associate of the Democratization Policy Council,12.02.2021
[134] Bodo Weber, Senior Associate of the Democratization Policy Council,15,02.2021
[135] Bodo Weber, Senior Associate of the Democratization Policy Council,12.02.2021

"Within such a clear framework for a final solution there is then hard work to do in negotiations over open, genuinely bilateral issues like missing persons, property issues, etc, where the Kosovan side will have to be ready to give something to Serbia, while Belgrade will have to restrain from misusing bilateral issues for reopening the status question."

- Kosovo's partition and an exchange of territories

"Any lobbying for partition, land swap etc is neither about Serbia's interests, let alone Kosovo Serb interests, but rather about traditionally conformist Balkan policy and the testing of a weakened West's resolve and red lines.

"Even in the case Vucic and [Kosovo President Hashim] Thaci agreed on such a dirty deal, no Kosovo Assembly would approve it with the necessary two-thirds majority. Not to speak about that any Western sanctioning of an ethno-territorial 'solution' would reopen Pandora's box in the region and beyond, and further destabilise Ukraine for example.

"It would even destabilise Serbia and Vucic, though he currently seems to be surprisingly unconscious about the potential consequences of his own policy.

"Finally, it perfectly demonstrates that Belgrade doesn't care about Kosovo Serbs as it has never done – the majority of Serbs live South of the Ibar – it just cares about continuing to pursue a conformist virtual, heavenly Kosovo policy as long as possible, instead of caring about the problems of the real Kosovo and the real Kosovo Serbs."*Answers have been edited for length and clarity.*

4.5.Fact and evidence in Kosovo

At Stake in this Election:

- 120 seats in the Assembly of Kosovo[136]

Government Structure:

- Chief of State: President Hashim Thaçi (since 7 April 2016)

---

[136] Constituion of Republic of Kosovo

- Head of Government: Prime Minister, Ramush Haradinaj, resigned on July 19, 2019 after being summoned for questioning by the Specialist Prosecutor's Office in The Hague. He remains as Acting Prime Minister until the October 6, 2019 elections
- Assembly: Unicameral Assembly (*Kuvendi i Kosoves/Skupstina Kosova*) with 120 seats.

Electoral System[137]:

- The President is elected by parliament to a 5-year term.
- 100 members of the Kosovar Assembly (*Kuvendi i Kosoves/Skupstina* [138]*Kosova*) are directly elected through a proportional representation vote with 20 seats reserved for ethnic minorities
    - 10 seats set aside for the representatives of the Serb community
    - 4 seats for the Roma, Ashkali and Egyptian communities (RAE)
    - 3 seats for the Bosniak community
    - 2 seats for the Turkish community
    - 1 seat for the Goran community
- All members serve 4-year terms.[139]
- In August 2019, Lawmakers in Kosovo voted to disband parliament to enable President Hashim Thaci to call early general elections following the resignation of Prime Minister Ramush Haradinaj. President Thaci was required to call the election within 45 days.

4.6.Main Parties in this Election:

On September 7th, the Election Commission published the official list of the 25 participating parties and coalitions. The official ballot can be found

- Party: Democratic Party of Kosovo / *Partia Demokratike e Kosovës* (PDK)
    - Leader: Kadri VESELI
    - Seats won in last election: 39
    - *Movement for Unification* candidates run inside PDK list.

[137] Constituion of Republic of Kosovo
[138] Constituion of Republic of Kosovo
[139] Constituion of Republic of Kosovo

- Party: Vetëvendosje (VV)!
    - Leader: Albin KURTI
    - Seats won in last election: 32
    - *Alternativa* candidates will run inside VV list.
- Party: Democratic League of Kosovo Lidhja Demokratike e Kosovës (LDK)
    - Leader: Isa MUSTAFA
    - Seats won in last election: 27
    - *Albanian Christian Democratic Party of Kosovo* (PSHDK) candidates will run inside the LDK list
- Coalition: Alliance for the Future of Kosovo (AAK) and Social Democratic Party of Kosovo (PSD)
    - Leader: Ramush HARADINAJ
    - Seats won in last election: 24
- Coalition: NISMA - AKR Coalition
    - Leader: Fatmir LIMAJ
    - Seats won in last election: 9
    - Includes the Social Democratic Initiative / *Nisma Social Demokrate* (NISMA); the New Kosovo Alliance / *Aleanca Kosova e Re* (AKR); and the Justice Party / Partia e Drejtësisë (PD).
- Party: Serbian Lista
    - Leader: Goran RAKIĆ
    - Seats won in last election: 9

Population and Registered Voters:

- Population: 1,907,592 (July 2018 est.)
- Registered Voters: 1,888,059

Gender Data:

- Female Population: 924,681
- Is Kosovo a signatory to CEDAW:
- Has Kosovo ratified CEDAW: No
- Gender Quota: No
- Female Candidates in this election: N/A
- Number of Female Legislators: 38
- Human Development Index (HDI) Position: N/A
- Social Institutions and Gender Index (SIGI) Categorization: N/A

Disability Data:

- Is Kosovo a signatory to CRPD: No
- Has Kosovo ratified CRPD: No
- Population with a disability: 280,647]

5.7.The CEC recounts 95 of the 314 polling stations[140]

The Central Election Commission is holding its next meeting. The meeting will report on the recount of the polling stations according to the CEC decision. There will also be reporting on the voting period by mail. Institute of Kosovo for Policy Development (IKPD) has demanded that 4500 packages of diaspora votes be counted in the counting system. According to the CEC preliminary results, the first party is the Vetevendosje Movement with 25.49 percent of the vote, followed by the Democratic League of Kosovo with 24.83 percent of the vote.

5.8.Diaspora votes [141]

"By mail came 15 thousand 795, over 3 thousand envelopes from Serbia, these envelopes were physically sent in the mail. Over 4 thousand envelopes Arrived after the deadline, during the verification we noticed that they were sent in international mail and hold the dates 19, 20 " September.

Some evidence according to the political situation in Kosovo

While the security situation in Kosovo remains broadly stable, government and political instability remains elevated. The Haradinaj government remains at constant risk of collapse, with early elections being only a matter of time. Pressure to revoke tariffs imposed by Pristina on goods coming from Bosnia and Serbia, along with talk of a possible land swap between Kosovo and Serbia as a way to resolve their mutual dispute over Kosovo's

---

[140] CEC,https://www.kqz-ks.org/zgjedhjet-e-pergjithshme/zgjedhjet-per-kuvend-te-kosoves-2019/

[141] CEC,https://www.kqz-ks.org/zgjedhjet-e-pergjithshme/zgjedhjet-per-kuvend-te-kosoves-2019/

statehood ,are all compounding political and societal splits and tensions within Kosovo[142].

Government Stability Kosovo's government continued to hover on the brink of collapse, given that it lacks a majority in the Kosovo Assembly. This situation has remained unchanged since the end of March 2018,when Srpska Lista, the block representing the ethnic Serb minority in the Assembly, announced that it would withdraw its support to the Kosovo government. In principle, this move reduced the Kosovo government's majority from around 61 MPs to 52 MPs in the 120 seat Assembly[143]. During the last three months, the government survived several key votes, including the adoption of legal changes aimed at transforming the Kosovo Security Forces (KSF) into an army in December, and the adoption of the 2019 budget on February 3. However, it would be misleading to conclude that these successful votes are a sign that the government commands some kind of majority[144]. On the contrary, the transformation of the KSF into an army was a matter of broad consensus among ethnic Albanian parties, while the passage of the 2019 budget was achieved thanks to the heavy conditioning and short-term calculations of the opposition Social Democrats (PSD). With these key votes out of the way, a number of parties in both the government and opposition may move further in the direction of deciding to bring down the government.[145] The Haradinaj government's predicament is further compounded by bitter disagreements between Prime Minister Ramush Haradinaj's Alliance for the Future of Kosovo (AAK) and the Democratic Partyof Kosovo (PDK) – formerly led by Kosovo President Hashim Thaci and now led by Parliamentary Speaker Kadri Veseli – over key policy areas.[146] To

142 Western BalkansStability Monitor https://consultancy.birn.eu.com/wp-content/uploads/2019/03/Western-Balkans-Stability-Monitor-March-2019.pdf

143 Western BalkansStability Monitor ,https://consultancy.birn.eu.com/wp-content/uploads/2019/03/Western-Balkans-Stability-Monitor-March-2019.pdf, pg25 14.10.2019

144Western BalkansStability Monitor, https://consultancy.birn.eu.com/wp-content/uploads/2019/03/Western-Balkans-Stability-Monitor-March-2019.pdf, pg25 14.10.2019

145 Western BalkansStability Monitor, https://consultancy.birn.eu.com/wp-content/uploads/2019/03/Western-Balkans-Stability-Monitor-March-2019.pdf, pg25 14.10.2019

146 Western BalkansStability Monitor, https://consultancy.birn.eu.com/wp-content/uploads/2019/03/Western-Balkans-Stability-Monitor-March-2019.pdf, pg25 14.10.2019

begin with, Thaci has emerged as a proponent of a deal with Belgrade which would involve an ethnically-based land swap between Kosovo and Serbia in return for mutual recognition.[147] The idea has been firmly opposed by Haradinaj and Veseli.[148] This conflict has been further compounded by the imposition of a 100%tariff on Bosnian and Serbian goods by Haradinaj's government, as retaliation against Serbia's lobbying for the de-recognition of Kosovo in a number of countries. Kosovo has come under strong pressure from the US and EU to revoke these tariffs, which have become an obstacle to the dialogue on normalizing relations between Belgrade and Pristina. While Thaci and Veseli. argue that Kosovo cannot risk losing support from its key international allies, Haradinaj has remained firm that he will not revoke the tariffs until Serbia recognizes Kosovo.[149]In reality, such behavior by both sides within the ruling coalition represents political posturing aimed at winning popular support ahead of early Parliamentary elections which will likely comeat some point in 2019. For the time being, neither the camp around Haradinaj, nor the camp around Thaci and Veseli seem willing to make a decisive move to bring down the government, hoping to capitalize further in terms of popular support.[150] Thaci and Veseli appear to be embroiled in a power struggle of their own for control of the PDK. Meanwhile, opposition political parties have their own – differing – political calculations, which ensure that there is – at present – no clear majority for bringing down the government.[151] Between its own internal divisions and its lack of a Parliamentary majority, the Kosovo government could fall at any moment. Yet in the absence of a clear will to bring it down immediately and the differing electoral calculations of rival political parties, the government

---

147 Western BalkansStability Monitor, https://consultancy.birn.eu.com/wp-content/uploads/2019/03/Western-Balkans-Stability-Monitor-March-2019.pdf, pg25 14.10.2019

[148] Western BalkansStability Monitor, https://consultancy.birn.eu.com/wp-content/uploads/2019/03/Western-Balkans-Stability-Monitor-March-2019.pdf, pg25 14.10.2019

149 Western BalkansStability Monitor, https://consultancy.birn.eu.com/wp-content/uploads/2019/03/Western-Balkans-Stability-Monitor-March-2019.pdf, pg25 14.10.2019

[150] Western BalkansStability Monitor, https://consultancy.birn.eu.com/wp-content/uploads/2019/03/Western-Balkans-Stability-Monitor-March-2019.pdf, pg25 14.10.2019

151Western BalkansStability Monitor, https://consultancy.birn.eu.com/wp-content/uploads/2019/03/Western-Balkans-Stability-Monitor-March-2019.pdf, pg25 14.10.2019

could limp on indefinitely. Nevertheless, the likelihood of early elections seems to rise with each passing week.[152]

6.After starting with great expectations, the EU-mediated dialogue process between Kosovo and Serbia is now stalled after the introduction by Prishtina of custom tariffs on Serbian products and sterile proposals to exchange territories

While the EU is striving to reach a Brexit deal with the UK, another peripheral problem – but with potential wider consequences – is keeping EU high officials busy: the stall in the "normalisation" dialogue between Kosovo and Serbia, which started 9 years ago, but has managed to deliver only a small part of the great expectations it initially fuelled.[153]

Last November, Kosovo's government dealt a last blow to the process by introducing a 100% tariff on imported Serbian goods, explaining the move as a reaction towards Serbia's de-recognition campaign and blocking Kosovo's membership to Interpol. Belgrade reacted immediately, interrupting the EU-mediated dialogue.[154]

"The EU has lost control of the process", says Florian Bieber, political scientist and professor at the University of Graz, Austria, working on inter-ethnic relations with focus on the Balkans. "The latest developments are part of the ongoing conflict for a final agreement, and things have become increasingly difficult as a result of earlier steps", he says. "The way the negotiation process was managed was not the right one for reaching a

---

152 Western BalkansStability Monitor, https://consultancy.birn.eu.com/wp-content/uploads/2019/03/Western-Balkans-Stability-Monitor-March-2019.pdf, pg25 14.10.2019

[153] Western BalkansStability Monitor, https://consultancy.birn.eu.com/wp-content/uploads/2019/03/Western-Balkans-Stability-Monitor-March-2019.pdf, pg25 14.10.2019

[154] Western BalkansStability Monitor, https://consultancy.birn.eu.com/wp-content/uploads/2019/03/Western-Balkans-Stability-Monitor-March-2019.pdf, pg25 14.10.2019

settlement between the parts, which would include some sort of recognition", says Bieber.[155]

Yet, according to Plamen Pantev, professor of International Relations Theory at the University of Sofia, Bulgaria, the EU has not failed in its long, persistent, and extensive efforts to pacify South East Europe. "Progress depends not only on the top-down activity, but mostly on the bottom-up evolution", he says, stressing the importance of the EU engagement in the region.[156]

"From a traditional transactional diplomacy point of view, the dialogue has not led to many significant changes, but it has been a considerable success in establishing a new relationship between Kosovo and Serbia", says former U.S. diplomat and Balkan expert James Hooper. According to Hooper, the Brussels agreement established sufficient trust between political leaders in Belgrade and Prishtina to enable both sides to raise their sights about what could be accomplished.[157]

10.1. Have the tariffs threatened Kosovo's relationship with its most important allies?

When it decided to introduce tariffs on Serbian imports, the Kosovo government acted without prior consultation with its main international allies – a rare move which led to some tensions with the United States and the European Union. According to Florian Bieber "these relations won't be hurt by Pristina showing some degree of independence, expecially having in mind that Kosovo is often eager to adjust to EU and U.S. positions", but he adds that "Kosovo needs to be careful and skilfull in managing such situations".[158] "The problem in Kosovo is the huge gap between the Prime Minister and the President: the government seems to be disunited, too, and

---

[155] Florian Bieber, professor for Southeast European History and Politics at the University of Graz and Coordinator of the Balkans in Europe Policy Advisory Group

[156] Florian Bieber, professor for Southeast European History and Politics at the University of Graz and Coordinator of the Balkans in Europe Policy Advisory Group

[157] Florian Bieber, professor for Southeast European History and Politics at the University of Graz and Coordinator of the Balkans in Europe Policy Advisory Group

[158] Western BalkansStability Monitor, https://consultancy.birn.eu.com/wp-content/uploads/2019/03/Western-Balkans-Stability-Monitor-March-2019.pdf, pg25 14.10.2019

this seriously weakens Kosovo's credibility on the international stage", he says.[159]

Former U.S. diplomat James Hooper, on the other hand, appears much more worried about the current political situation in Kosovo. He considers the behaviour of some Kosovo political leaders as a sign of provincialism rather than stubborness. He recalls that since the 2016 elections the US policy has been less committed to support Kosovo. "In this new situation, Kosovars need to work even harder to maintain a strong relationship with the US. But, because of the narrow – in my opinion, provincial – way some politicians look at Kosovo's interests, they are not able to perceive the dangerous position in which they are placing their country", says Hooper, who has covered from Washington D.C. the Rambouillet peace agreement 1999. According to Hooper, the US-Kosovo relationship is at its lowest since the NATO-led war against Yugoslavia 20 years ago, and this is a direct result of tariffs.[160]

"100% tariffs are not part of Prishtina's economic philosophy, but are being used as a tool to put pressure on Belgrade", Professor Plamen Pantev says, adding that it is a clear signal "that bilateral relations need a restart".[161]

10.2.Is partition the solution?

Leaders from both Serbia and Kosovo realised that they were on the threshold of a new phase of the bilateral dialogue when they started to openly discuss the possibility of partition and land swapping, a discussion which was not initiated by the EU, but which Brussels had to eventually acknowledge as an option on the table. However, voices against any border changes remain strong.[162]

---

[159] Florian Bieber, professor for Southeast European History and Politics at the University of Graz and Coordinator of the Balkans in Europe Policy Advisory Group

[160] Western BalkansStability Monitor, https://consultancy.birn.eu.com/wp-content/uploads/2019/03/Western-Balkans-Stability-Monitor-March-2019.pdf, pg25 14.10.2019

[161] Western BalkansStability Monitor, https://consultancy.birn.eu.com/wp-content/uploads/2019/03/Western-Balkans-Stability-Monitor-March-2019.pdf, pg25 14.10.2019

[162] Western BalkansStability Monitor, https://consultancy.birn.eu.com/wp-content/uploads/2019/03/Western-Balkans-Stability-Monitor-March-2019.pdf, pg25 14.10.2019

"The biggest problem, however, arises from the fact that the annexation of Crimea by the Russian Federation in 2014 reinforced negative perceptions of any territorial change", says Professor Pantev, adding that the problem is also linked to Moscow's policy towards Serbia, preventing Belgrade from finding a solution to its Kosovo issue in a constructive way. "Russia does not want that", he says.[163]

Serbia needs an agreement with Kosovo to advance its EU candidacy, and Kosovo needs Serbia to be in the EU, where it will become subject to EU constraints on its military, security, and foreign policy actions, says Hooper. "I see the delineation of the border between Kosovo and Serbia as not only a stabilising factor, but an essential one for the greater stability of the Balkan region. It is important for Kosovars to understand that territory is a means to an end – a greater security for an independent Kosovo, not a goal in itself".

As the dialogue reaches its final stage, there will be a need for the solution to be legal and in line with international law. The final settlement will have to ensure that it does not endanger regional stability and that it does not negatively affect the communities involved, says Florian Bieber. "These are the key red lines that need to be set. Border changes, though, by definition, are not able to deliver on that, because they cannot provide regional stability and security". There is a grey zone in which negotiation is possible, but overall, "border changes in the way suggested by presidents of both countries are quite problematic", says Bieber.[164]

Current EU High Representative for Foreign Affairs and Security Policy Federica Mogherini is at the end of her mandate, so new negotiations will have to rely on the new European Commission which will emerge after the European elections, scheduled for next May. Probably, the process will not actually resume before the end of 2019.[165]

After fighting broke out between government forces and separatists, the formerly Serbian province of Kosovo was transferred to United Nations

---

[163] Florian Bieber, professor for Southeast European History and Politics at the University of Graz and Coordinator of the Balkans in Europe Policy Advisory Group

[164] Florian Bieber, professor for Southeast European History and Politics at the University of Graz and Coordinator of the Balkans in Europe Policy Advisory Group

[165] Florian Bieber, professor for Southeast European History and Politics at the University of Graz and Coordinator of the Balkans in Europe Policy Advisory Group

administration in 1999. In 2008, Kosovo declared independence. However, Belgrade continues to view its former province as Serbian territory. Over 100 countries, including 23 EU Member States, have recognized Kosovar independence, but full recognition and membership of most international organizations are still a long way off[166].Both Serbia and Kosovo aspire to EU membership – Serbia as a candidate country and Kosovo as a potential candidate[167]. The EU insists that Serbia must normalise its relations with Kosovo before joining. Since 2011, with the help of EU mediation, the two neighbours have resolved some of the technical issues, but disagreements prevent normal day-to-day interaction between them in areas such as trade, energy supplies and cross-border travel. One of the main stumbling blocks is the situation of Kosovo's Serb minority. Around one in 12 Kosovars is an ethnic Serb, and nearly half of these are concentrated in the north[168]. Despite efforts to integrate Serb-majority northern Kosovo into the rest of the country, Pristina still struggles to control the region. In 2013 and 2015, it agreed to establish an Association of Serb-majority Municipalities, but progress on this is now dead locked[169]. In 2018, the Kosovar and Serbian presidents floated the idea of a 'border correction', possibly involving the exchange of northern Kosovo for Albanian-majority Serbian districts. However, the proposal has been criticised by Germany, which fears that any territorial exchange risks sparking instability by calling into question other Western Balkan borders[170]. There is also strong domestic opposition to the move in both Kosovo and Serbia.Despite growing pressure on both sides to

---

[166]European Parliament, briefing, Serbia-Kosovo relationsConfrontation or normalisation? http://www.europarl.europa.eu/RegData/etudes/BRIE/2019/635512/EPRS_BRI(2019)635512_EN.pdfhttp://www.europarl.europa.eu/RegData/etudes/BRIE/2019/635512/EPRS_BRI(2019)635512_EN.pdf

[167] European Parliament, briefing Serbia-Kosovo relationsConfrontation or normalisation? http://www.europarl.europa.eu/RegData/etudes/BRIE/2019/635512/EPRS_BRI(2019)635512_EN.pdf

[168] Serbia-Kosovo relationsConfrontation or normalisation? http://www.europarl.europa.eu/RegData/etudes/BRIE/2019/635512/EPRS_BRI(2019)635512_EN.pdf

European Parliament, briefing [169] Serbia-Kosovo relationsConfrontation or normalisation? http://www.europarl.europa.eu/RegData/etudes/BRIE/2019/635512/EPRS_BRI(2019)635512_EN.pdf

[170] European Parliament, briefing, Serbia-Kosovo relationsConfrontation or normalisation? http://www.europarl.europa.eu/RegData/etudes/BRIE/2019/635512/EPRS_BRI(2019)635512_EN.pdfhttp://www.europarl.europa.eu/RegData/etudes/BRIE/2019/635512/EPRS_BRI(2019)635512_EN.pdf

finally reach a deal that could unlock the door to EU membership, relations remain tense and progress towards normalisation is currently at a standstill.The (currently blocked) Mitrovica Bridge in Kosovo.In this Briefing Timeline The EU's role in Serbia-Kosovo relationsSerbia-Kosovo agreements on technical issuesSituation of the Kosovan Serb minorityPolitical obstacles to normalisationOutlook: zero-sum or win-win?

10.3.History chronology of Kosovo

1999-2008: Kosovo became a provisionally self-governed territory under UN administration. In 2007, a plan for Kosovar independence negotiated by former Finnish President, Martti Ahtisaari, was rejected by Serbia.2008: Kosovo's unilateral declaration of independence was recognised by most European countries and the United States.2010: the International Court of Justice ruled that Kosovo's declaration of independence is not in conflict with international law.2011: direct EU-mediated talks between Serbia and Kosovo began for the first time since the latter's declaration of independence.2011-2015: as a result of the EU talks, Serbia and Kosovo concluded a number of important agreements, including the Brussels Agreement (April 2013).Since 2015, little progress has been made on reaching new agreements or on implementing the ones previously concluded. A series of confrontations has brought relations to a new low.

January 2017: a Serbian train decorated with the words 'Kosovo is Serbia' in 21 languages headed for the Serb-majority Kosovar town of North Mitrovica, causing outrage in Kosovo. January-

August 2018: Kosovar and Serbian presidents, Hashim Thaçi and Aleksandar Vučić, floated the idea of a 'border correction' as a way out of their impasse, but the proposal quickly ran into opposition.

November 2018: Kosovo brought in 10 % customs duties on imports from Serbia, subsequently raised to 100 %, after Serbia blocked Kosovo's efforts to join Interpol. December 2018: Kosovo decided to upgrade its security force into a fully-fledged army. Although the Kosovar army will be small with just 5 000 troops, Serbia sees it as a threat and has warned that the move could trigger a military response.

10.4.The EU's role in Serbia-Kosovo relations

Brussels has long been a key player in Kosovo. In 2008, the EU rule of law mission in Kosovo (EULEX, a civilian mission under the EU's common security and defence policy), took over police, justice and customs functions from the United Nations. Now that Kosovo has developed its own institutions, most of these tasks have since been transferred to the Kosovar authorities, but EULEX continues to monitor the rule of law in Kosovo and will remain in the country at least until June 2020[171].The EU is Kosovo's largest aid donor, with nearly €650 million of funding from the Instrument for Pre-accession Assistance[172]. A large share (€237 million) has been earmarked to support rule of law and other reforms to prepare Kosovo for possible EU membership. Since 2011, the EU has also played a crucial role in mediating direct talks between Serbia and Kosovo (the 'EU-facilitated dialogue'), aimed at normalizing relations between the two sides. During the first year of the dialogue, talks were held at technical level, but from October 2012 they were upgraded Serbia-Kosovo relations to political level, with meetings between the Serbian and Kosovar prime ministers[173]. The dialogue initially scored a series of successes: 33 agreements, mostly on technical issues but also including the ambitious but vague Brussels Agreement of April 2013 and, in August 2015, a text on the thorny issue of Serb-majority northern Kosovo. Since 2016, dialogue has stalled, with several meetings delayed or cancelled and little progress on implementing previous commitments or on concluding new agreements. The tone of the meetings has become increasingly acrimonious, with repeated threats by both sides to pull out of dialogue[174]. At the meeting scheduled in Brussels for September 2018, President Vučić refused to meet President Thaçi; the two leaders eventually met two months later, but shortly afterwards Vučić announced that there would be no further dialogue until Kosovo lifted its 100 % duties on Serbian imports. Both Serbia and Kosovo aspire to join the

---

[171] European Parliament, briefing, Serbia-Kosovo relationsConfrontation or normalisation? http://www.europarl.europa.eu/RegData/etudes/BRIE/2019/635512/EPRS_BRI(2019)635512_EN.pdfhttp://www.europarl.europa.eu/RegData/etudes/BRIE/2019/635512/EPRS_BRI(2019)635512_EN.pdf

[172] European Parliament, briefing, Serbia-Kosovo relationsConfrontation or normalisation? http://www.europarl.europa.eu/RegData/etudes/BRIE/2019/635512/EPRS_BRI(2019)635512_EN.pdfhttp://www.europarl.europa.eu/RegData/etudes/BRIE/2019/635512/EPRS_BRI(2019)635512_EN.pdf

[173] European Parliament, briefing, Serbia-Kosovo relationsConfrontation or normalisation? http://www.europarl.europa.eu/RegData/etudes/BRIE/2019/635512/EPRS_BRI(2019)635512_EN.pdfhttp://www.europarl.europa.eu/RegData/etudes/BRIE/2019/635512/EPRS_BRI(2019)635512_EN.pdf

[174] European Parliament, briefing, Serbia-Kosovo relationsConfrontation or normalisation? http://www.europarl.europa.eu/RegData/etudes/BRIE/2019/635512/EPRS_BRI(2019)635512_EN.pdfhttp://www.europarl.europa.eu/RegData/etudes/BRIE/2019/635512/EPRS_BRI(2019)635512_EN.pdf

EU, and Serbia has been a candidate since 2012. The main incentive which the EU can offer the two sides to keep talking is the prospect of eventual EU membership – for Serbia, perhaps as early as in 2025. The EU has made Serbian membership conditional on resolving the Kosovo issue. The January 2014 negotiating framework for Serbia states explicitly that the two sides must sign a legally binding agreement enabling 'comprehensive normalization of relations' by the end of the accession process. The same document also specifies that the EU can decide not to open new negotiating chapters if Serbia fails to implement its agreements with Pristina in good faith. Conversely, the EU can reward both countries for progress towards normalization, as it did in 2015, by signing a stabilization and association agreement (SAA) with Kosovo and opening accession negotiations with Serbia. The fact that progress has stalled despite such incentives suggests that domestic political pressures outweigh the still distant prospect of future EU membership. In 2018, just 29 % of Serbians declared themselves in favor of EU membership, less than in any other Western Balkan country. At the same time, 81 % of Serbs are against recognizing Kosovo's independence, even in exchange for faster EU membership; 63 % see a frozen conflict as the best possible outcome; and just 21 % support an agreement with Pristina. With Vučić under pressure from opposition protests accusing him of authoritarian tendencies and the possibility of early elections being called in 2019, he is unlikely to make unpopular concessions on Kosovo.Kosovo's minority government is even less likely to go against public opinion. Polls from 2018 suggest that Kosovars are highly supportive of EU membership (84 %), but also that there is much less enthusiasm for dialogue with Serbia; 52 % and 77 % respectively of Kosovar Albanians and Serbs are skeptical that dialogue with Serbia could benefit their lives, and 52 % of the country's population are in favors of suspending talks with Belgrade, regardless of the international consequences[175].

Serbia-Kosovo relations to political level, with meetings between the Serbian and Kosovar prime ministers. The dialogue initially scored a series of successes: 33 agreements, mostly on technical issues but also including the ambitious but vague Brussels Agreement of April 2013 and, in August 2015, a text on the thorny issue of Serb-majority northern Kosovo.Since 2016, dialogue has stalled, with several meetings delayed or cancelled and

---

175 European Parliament, briefing, Serbia-Kosovo relationsConfrontation or normalisation? http://www.europarl.europa.eu/RegData/etudes/BRIE/2019/635512/EPRS_BRI(2019)635512_EN.pdfhttp://www.europarl.europa.eu/RegData/etudes/BRIE/2019/635512/EPRS_BRI(2019)635512_EN.pdf

little progress on implementing previous commitments or on concluding new agreements. The tone of the meetings has become increasingly acrimonious, with repeated threats by both sides to pull out of dialogue[176]. At the meeting scheduled in Brussels for September 2018, President Vučić refused to meet President Thaçi; the two leaders eventually met two months later, but shortly afterwards Vučić announced that there would be no further dialogue until Kosovo lifted its 100 % duties on Serbian imports. Both Serbia and Kosovo aspire to join the EU, and Serbia has been a candidate since 2012. The main incentive which the EU can offer the two sides to keep talking is the prospect of eventual EU membership – for Serbia, perhaps as early as in 2025. The EU has made Serbian membership conditional on resolving the Kosovo issue. The January 2014 negotiating framework for Serbia states explicitly that the two sides must sign a legally binding agreement enabling 'comprehensive normalization of relations' by the end of the accession process. The same document also specifies that the EU can decide not to open new negotiating chapters if Serbia fails to implement its agreements with Pristina in good faith. Conversely, the EU can reward both countries for progress towards normalization, as it did in 2015, by signing a stabilization and association agreement (SAA) with Kosovo and opening accession negotiations with Serbia. The fact that progress has stalled despite such incentives suggests that domestic political pressures outweigh the still distant prospect of future EU membership. In 2018, just 29 % of Serbians declared themselves in favour of EU membership, less than in any other Western Balkan country. At the same time, 81 % of Serbs are against recognizing Kosovo's independence, even in exchange for faster EU membership; 63 % see a frozen conflict as the best possible outcome; and just 21 % support an agreement with Pristina. With Vučić under pressure from opposition protests accusing him of authoritarian tendencies and the possibility of early elections being called in 2019, he is unlikely to make unpopular concessions on Kosovo.Kosovo's minority government is even less likely to go against public opinion. Polls from 2018 suggest that Kosovars are highly supportive of EU membership (84 %), but also that there is much less enthusiasm for dialogue with Serbia; 52 % and 77 % respectively of Kosovar Albanians and Serbs are skeptical that dialogue with Serbia could benefit their lives, and 52 % of the country's

---

[176] European Parliament, briefing, Serbia-Kosovo relationsConfrontation or normalisation? http://www.europarl.europa.eu/RegData/etudes/BRIE/2019/635512/EPRS_BRI(2019)635512_EN.pdfhttp://www.europarl.europa.eu/RegData/etudes/BRIE/2019/635512/EPRS_BRI(2019)635512_EN.pdf

population are in favour of suspending talks with Belgrade, regardless of the international consequences[177].

10.5.Serbia-Kosovo agreements on technical issues

Given the impasse resulting from Serbia's refusal to recognize Kosovo, negotiations in the early stages of the EU-facilitated dialogue focused on mostly technical arrangements for day-to-day relations between the two sides[178]. In numerical terms, considerable progress was made, with 33 agreements in total concluded. However, implementation of many of these has been slow and incomplete, creating practical problems in a wide range of areas[179].Trade: since 2007, both Serbia and Kosovo have been committed to duty-free bilateral trade, as part of the central European free-trade area[180]. A trade embargo between the two sides ended in 2011, when Serbia agreed to accept goods stamped 'Kosovo customs', with no national coat of arms or flag. In 2017, Serbia accounted for 12 % of Kosovo's foreign trade. However, in November 2018 economic relations ran into another obstacle: two weeks after imposing 10 % tariffs on imports from Serbia for the latter's campaign against international recognition of Kosovo, Pristina raised tariffs to 100 %, after Serbia allegedly blocked its bid to join Interpol. The measure is estimated to cost Serbia around €40 million a month in lost exports. Resisting strong EU and US pressure to drop the tariffs, Kosovo has pledged to keep them in place until it is recognized by Serbia; (it has since slightly softened its stance, demanding instead 'an international guarantee' of talks leading to mutual recognition)[181]. Telecommunications has been

---

[177] European Parliament, briefing, Serbia-Kosovo relationsConfrontation or normalisation? http://www.europarl.europa.eu/RegData/etudes/BRIE/2019/635512/EPRS_BRI(2019)635512_EN.pdfhttp://www.europarl.europa.eu/RegData/etudes/BRIE/2019/635512/EPRS_BRI(2019)635512_EN.pdf

[178] European Parliament, briefing, Serbia-Kosovo relationsConfrontation or normalisation? http://www.europarl.europa.eu/RegData/etudes/BRIE/2019/635512/EPRS_BRI(2019)635512_EN.pdfhttp://www.europarl.europa.eu/RegData/etudes/BRIE/2019/635512/EPRS_BRI(2019)635512_EN.pdf

[179] European Parliament, briefing, Serbia-Kosovo relationsConfrontation or normalisation? http://www.europarl.europa.eu/RegData/etudes/BRIE/2019/635512/EPRS_BRI(2019)635512_EN.pdfhttp://www.europarl.europa.eu/RegData/etudes/BRIE/2019/635512/EPRS_BRI(2019)635512_EN.pdf

[180] European Parliament, briefing, Serbia-Kosovo relationsConfrontation or normalisation? http://www.europarl.europa.eu/RegData/etudes/BRIE/2019/635512/EPRS_BRI(2019)635512_EN.pdfhttp://www.europarl.europa.eu/RegData/etudes/BRIE/2019/635512/EPRS_BRI(2019)635512_EN.pdf

[181] European Parliament, briefing, Serbia-Kosovo relationsConfrontation or normalisation? http://www.europarl.europa.eu/RegData/etudes/BRIE/2019/635512/EPRS_BRI(2019)6355

one of the more positive areas: an agreement reached in 2016 gives Kosovo its own international dialing code, while allowing a subsidiary of Serbia's state-owned Telekom Serbia to continue operating in Kosovo. Regional representation and cooperation: initially, Kosovo was represented in (mostly EU-led) regional for a by the UN's Mission in Kosovo. In 2012, Serbia agreed that Kosovo could act on its own behalf, provided that it designates itself as Kosovo* with the accompanying footnote: 'This designation is without prejudice to positions on status, and is in line with UNSCR 1244/1999 and the ICJ Opinion on the Kosovo declaration of independence'[182]. Border/boundary crossings: to improve border security and reduce waiting times, in 2012 the two sides agreed to upgrade the six existing border (or as Serbia has it, boundary) crossings between them, following the integrated border management approach used by the EU for its external borders. The new crossings will be neutral in appearance, displaying no state symbols. However, construction has only progressed at two of the six. Freedom of movement: a 2011 agreement allows Kosovars to travel into Serbia with identity documents issued by Pristina, and vice-versa, and a further agreement in 2015 establishes mutual recognition of car insurance. However, the two sides do not recognize one another's car number plates and require cross-border drivers to purchase temporary plates. The problem was supposed to have been solved by a 2016 agreement, under which Kosovar drivers can paste stickers over the offending parts of their number plates (on similar lines to the approach taken by Greece for cars from the former Yugoslav Republic of Macedonia, prior to the Prespa Agreement), but this has yet to be implemented. Although Belgrade and Pristina are just 300 km apart, there are no direct flights or trains between them.

Energy: European grid operators are obliged to help neighboring countries cover their needs in the event of a shortfall. Despite signing an energy agreement with Kosovo in 2015, Serbia refused to meet its supply obligations to Pristina in March 2018, disrupting the grid not only in Kosovo but also throughout Europe. Serbia also does not pay Kosovo for the use of its interconnection lines; Pristina claims this has cost it €52 million in lost revenue since 2008. Normalization of relations with Kosovo is a condition

---

12_EN.pdfhttp://www.europarl.europa.eu/RegData/etudes/BRIE/2019/635512/EPRS_BRI(2019)635512_EN.pdf

[182] European Parliament, briefing, Serbia-Kosovo relationsConfrontation or normalisation? http://www.europarl.europa.eu/RegData/etudes/BRIE/2019/635512/EPRS_BRI(2019)635512_EN.pdfhttp://www.europarl.europa.eu/RegData/etudes/BRIE/2019/635512/EPRS_BRI(2019)635512_EN.pdf

for Serbia to join the EU, but Brussels does not explicitly demand recognition; the Belgrade government's position is that the two issues should be kept separate[183]. Theoretically, the two countries could indeed agree on an arrangement that would unblock Kosovo's recognition by other countries and its EU membership, without requiring full formal recognition by Serbia – perhaps something on the lines of the 1972 Basic Treaty between the two halves of Germany. However, given that Kosovo also hopes to join the EU, it is difficult to imagine that the two countries could co-exist as Member States without mutual recognition. Border readjustment as a way out of the impasse? At an August 2018 meeting in Austria, Serbia's and Kosovo's presidents were in rare agreement on a tentative suggestion that 'border correction' could be a way forward to improved relations. Although the nature of the correction was not specified, it is widely assumed that the two leaders had in mind a handover of Serb-majority northern Kosovo to Belgrade; in exchange, Kosovo could gain Albanian-majority districts in the PreševoValley adjacent to its southern border[184].On the face of it, a land swap arrangement would offer several advantages. It would resolve the status of northern Kosovo, and would also address complaints of discrimination against Serbia's Albanian minority. Most importantly, such a deal could open the door to a broader agreement normalizing relations between the two sides. The United States and Austria have expressed openness to the idea, as has EU High Representative Federica Mogherini[185]. On the other hand, there are also serious

---

[183] European Parliament, briefing, Serbia-Kosovo relationsConfrontation or normalisation? http://www.europarl.europa.eu/RegData/etudes/BRIE/2019/635512/EPRS_BRI(2019)635512_EN.pdfhttp://www.europarl.europa.eu/RegData/etudes/BRIE/2019/635512/EPRS_BRI(2019)635512_EN.pdf

European Parliament, briefing, Serbia-Kosovo relationsConfrontation or normalisation? http://www.europarl.europa.eu/RegData/etudes/BRIE/2019/635512/EPRS_BRI(2019)635512_EN.pdfhttp://www.europarl.europa.eu/RegData/etudes/BRIE/2019/635512/EPRS_BRI(2019)635512_EN.pdf

[184] European Parliament, briefing, Serbia-Kosovo relationsConfrontation or normalisation? http://www.europarl.europa.eu/RegData/etudes/BRIE/2019/635512/EPRS_BRI(2019)635512_EN.pdfhttp://www.europarl.europa.eu/RegData/etudes/BRIE/2019/635512/EPRS_BRI(2019)635512_EN.pdf

[185] European Parliament, briefing, Serbia-Kosovo relationsConfrontation or normalisation? http://www.europarl.europa.eu/RegData/etudes/BRIE/2019/635512/EPRS_BRI(2019)635512_EN.pdfhttp://www.europarl.europa.eu/RegData/etudes/BRIE/2019/635512/EPRS_BRI(2019)635512_EN.pdf

objections[186]. A partition of Kosovo on ethnic lines could call into question borders of other multi-ethnic states, such as Bosnia and Herzegovina, potentially even threatening the region's fragile peace. Germany and the UK are among the most vocal opponents, as are regional neighbors, such as Albania and Montenegro[187]. The Serbian Orthodox Church opposes a potential deal, arguing that Serbia, by accepting northern Kosovo, would give up its claims to the rest of the country. Unsurprisingly, given that Pristina stands to lose more than it gains, Kosovar resistance is even stronger: northern Kosovo includes strategic assets such as the Trepca mine as well as the Gazivoda reservoir supplying Pristina with drinking water, whereas the Albanian-majority areas that Kosovo could potentially receive in return are smaller and have little industry. President Thaçi is the only senior Kosovar figure to have expressed support for the idea; government and opposition parties have been against it from the start, and in November 2018 even Thaçi appeared to back-track, denying that any border corrections on ethnic lines were being considered. Not even the country's Serb minority is fully behind ethnic partition, due to fears that the transfer of northern Kosovo would isolate the remaining half of the Kosovar Serb population living in enclaves scattered across the rest of the country.

10.6. Zero-sum or win-win?

In the early stages of the EU-mediated talks between Serbia and Kosovo that began in 2011, negotiators focused on practical problems, in the hope that success in resolving these would build trust and create more conducive conditions for tackling more divisive political subjects such as Kosovar Serb autonomy. For a while, this approach seemed to work, delivering a series of agreements that culminated in the 2013 Brussels Agreement and the subsequent 2015 agreement on an Association of Serb Municipalities. However, since then the process has ground to a halt. Even on technical issues (such as electricity grids and car registration) the two sides are at

---

[186] European Parliament, briefing, Serbia-Kosovo relationsConfrontation or normalisation? http://www.europarl.europa.eu/RegData/etudes/BRIE/2019/635512/EPRS_BRI(2019)635512_EN.pdfhttp://www.europarl.europa.eu/RegData/etudes/BRIE/2019/635512/EPRS_BRI(2019)635512_EN.pdf

[187] European Parliament, briefing, Serbia-Kosovo relationsConfrontation or normalisation? http://www.europarl.europa.eu/RegData/etudes/BRIE/2019/635512/EPRS_BRI(2019)635512_EN.pdfhttp://www.europarl.europa.eu/RegData/etudes/BRIE/2019/635512/EPRS_BRI(2019)635512_EN.pdf

loggerheads. A solution to the trickier political challenges seems further away than ever, with neither side willing to make concessions, even in exchange for EU membership. The border adjustment floated in 2018 temporarily raised hopes of a possible way forward, but domestic and international opposition to the idea appears insuperable. Although both Kosovar and Serbian leaders acknowledge that they need to keep talking, there is little sign of openness to compromise. In 2015, both Serbia and Kosovo presented the four agreements concluded during EU-mediated talks as a defeat for the other side; for then-Prime Minister Thaçi, Kosovo had effectively forced Serbia to recognize it as an independent state, while Serbian representative, Marko Djurić, hailed a '5-0 victory' for Belgrade. A similar zero-sum logic prevails in Serbian Interior Minister Nebojsa Stefanovic's tweet welcoming Interpol's 2018 rejection of Kosovo's membership bid as a 'victory', and in the ongoing squabbles over alleged recognition or non-recognition of Kosovo by third countries. Both Thaçi and the US administration seem confident that 2019 could finally bring a comprehensive agreement. However, so long as confrontational attitudes continue, the compromises needed for this to happen seem unlikely[188].

10.7.Opposition Activities

While the opposition parties in the Kosovo Assembly clearly have the necessary votes to bring down the Haradinaj government, they remain divided and unwilling to cooperate and coordinate. As such, they remain the best 'ally' for the Haradinaj cabinet's efforts to hold on to power a little longer. The key question remains which of the opposition parties in the Kosovo Parliament really wish to bring down the Haradinaj government at present, in doing so forcing early elections. As with the parties of the ruling coalition, some in the opposition are clearly more interested in short-term ways of boosting their popular support before any early elections. Although Srpska Lista left the governing coalition in the spring, until recently it seemed unwilling to actually bring the Haradinaj government down, due to its own – and Belgrade's – political calculations. This deprived the

---

[188] European Parliament, briefing, Serbia-Kosovo relationsConfrontation or normalisation? http://www.europarl.europa.eu/RegData/etudes/BRIE/2019/635512/EPRS_BRI(2019)635512_EN.pdfhttp://www.europarl.europa.eu/RegData/etudes/BRIE/2019/635512/EPRS_BRI(2019)635512_EN.pdf

opposition parties of the votes needed to bring the government down. Following the imposition of tariffs on Serbian goods in November, this situation changed radically – Srpska Lista now appears willing to vote against the Haradinaj government, but other, more nationalist, opposition parties such as Self-determination have made it clear that they will not cooperate with Srpska Lista – and Belgrade by extension – to bring down Haradinaj's government over the tariff issue on which they – and their voters – essentially support Haradinaj's stance. While Self-determination and the Democratic League of Kosovo (LDK) do not wish to cooperate with Srpska Lista in bringing the government down, they have also proven unwilling to lend ittheir support. However, this has not been the case with the PSD, which has flirted with supporting the government. The PSD recently joined the newly-formed Kosovo Negotiating Team, albeit as representatives of the opposition – after the LDK and Self-determination had refused to do so, as the bigger opposition parties. PSD leader Spend Ahmeti is now one of the'co-leaders' of the negotiating team. Similarly, the PSD voted in favour of the adoption of the2019 budget, albeit conditioning its support with demands such as the dismissal of Nenad Rikalo, until recently the Kosovo Serb Minister of Agriculture, from the government. At present,the PSD claims that it is using its sporadic support as a lever to bring about specific positive changes. Although some observers have speculated that the PSD might actually join the ruling coalition, this seems unlikely at present. Rather, the PSD – which, with its 12 MPs, in 2018 split from Self-determination - is likely still unprepared for competing in an early election and hopes that its man oeuvres will buy it both time and popular support in an inevitable early election. In such a climate, LDK deputy leader Agim Veliu proposed some form of government of national consensus, which would include all the parties in the Kosovo Parliament. Accordingly, the government would have a clear time limit to its life after which elections would be called and the task of completing several important tasks, including the dialogue with Serbia, as well as preparing constitutional and electoral reforms. Yet in a climate where all parties seem to be23 jockeying for prime positions ahead of early elections, such an idea seems to have little chance of success at present.

CHAPTER II

1.Regional Relations

Relations between Kosovo and Serbia remained poor, following the decision of Pristina to impose a 100% tariff on Serbian and Bosnian goods in November. Belgrade has made it clear that the Brussels-mediated dialogue will remain suspended until Pristina revokes the tariff. Meanwhile, Kosovo Prime Minister Ramush Haradinaj has declared that the tariffs will only beremoved once Serbia recognizes Kosovo. In an effort to break this stalemate, US and European diplomats have exerted pressure on Pristina to revoke the tariffs, or at least temporarily suspend them, making it clear that the course charted by Kosovo's government was undermining its relationship with key allies. While Kosovo's President Hashim Thaci has stressed the need to respect the advice of Kosovo's key allies, Haradinaj has dug his heels in, refusing to revoke the tariffs[189]. The idea that Serbia might recognize Kosovo in order to secure the removal of the tariffs is clearly a non-starter, something that Pristina is well aware of[190]. This then begs the question if Pristina might settle for some other concession in return for lifting the tariff. In the short term, there is nothing to suggest that this particular dispute between Belgrade and Pristina will be resolved, unless the international community significantly steps up pressure on Pristina. In the meantime, rumours abound that Kosovo and Serbia – or, more precisely, Presidents Hashim Thaci and Aleksandar Vucic and their representatives – are deep in negotiations over the idea of a land-swap deal which would see the Serb populated north of Kosovo ceded to Serbia, while ethnic Albanian populated villages in southern Serbia would be ceded to Kosovo. Any such deal would also involve some form of mutual recognition between Kosovo and Serbia. While the negotiations on a deal seem to be in an advanced phase, it remains particularly unclear how Thaci would be able to sell such a deal in Kosovo, given stiff opposition to any agreement involving a land-swap among most political parties in Kosovo. Indeed, the official Kosovo Negotiating Team adopted a negotiating platform in mid-February with a clear statement that the territory of Kosovo could not be altered.24

---

[189] Western BalkansStability Monitor ,https://consultancy.birn.eu.com/wp-content/uploads/2019/03/Western-Balkans-Stability-Monitor-March-2019.pdf, pg25 14.10.2019

190Western BalkansStability Monitor, https://consultancy.birn.eu.com/wp-content/uploads/2019/03/Western-Balkans-Stability-Monitor-March-2019.pdf, pg25 14.10.2019

Kosovo's relations with its other neighbors remained uneventful. Albanian Prime Minister Edi Rama was among the foreign leaders in attendance at the Kosovo independence celebrations in Pristina on February 17. Faced with student protests in Albania, Rama attempted to placate critics by sacking seven ministers in his government. It was notable that he proposed two ethnic Albanian citizens of Kosovo as the new ministers for education and foreign affairs. Montenegrin President Milos Djukanovic met with Kosovo PM Ramush Haradinaj on the margins of the Munich Security Conference in February, exchanging pleasantries and expressions ofmutual support. On February 21, Kadri Veseli, the Speaker of Kosovo's Parliament and leader of the ruling PDK, called on Montenegro and North Macedonia to form an alliance against Serbia. The idea was immediately dismissed by Montenegrin Prime Minister Dusko Markovic as nonsense[191].

1.1Security

On December 14, Kosovo's government successfully passed several laws intended to transform the Kosovo Security Force (KSF) into an army. From now on, Kosovo will formally have a Ministry of Defense, while the mandate of the KSF has been expanded and the ground prepared for internal organization. In reality, the vote was the beginning, rather than the end, of the process of transforming the KSF into an army[192]. Not least of the hurdles Kosovo will need to surmount willbe changing the constitution in order to fully enact this transformation, something that requires both an ordinary two-thirds majority in the Kosovo Parliament and a two-thirds majority amongMPs representing ethnic minorities[193].

While such support for constitutional amendments is unlikely to materialize in the short-term, the2019 Kosovo budget increased the funding for the Ministry of Defense – and by extension KSF– by around six million euros in order to enable the KSF's transition to an army[194]. The KSF was also out in

191Western BalkansStability Monitor https://consultancy.birn.eu.com/wp-content/uploads/2019/03/Western-Balkans-Stability-Monitor-March-2019.pdf, pg25 14.10.2019

192Western BalkansStability Monitor https://consultancy.birn.eu.com/wp-content/uploads/2019/03/Western-Balkans-Stability-Monitor-March-2019.pdf,14.10.2019

193 https://consultancy.birn.eu.com/wp-content/uploads/2019/03/Western-Balkans-Stability-Monitor-March-2019.pdf,14.10.2019

194 https://consultancy.birn.eu.com/wp-content/uploads/2019/03/Western-Balkans-Stability-Monitor-March-2019.pdf, pg25 14.10.2019

force during Kosovo's independence day celebrations, organizing a military parade on the occasion[195]. At the same time, a planned visit from the US Iowa National Guard commander, Major General Timothy Orr, to the KSF on February 16-18 was cancelled due to Kosovo's failure to revoke the tariff on Serbian and Bosnian goods. KSF commander Rrahman Rama stated that he had been warned by US officials that other forms of cooperation with the Iowa National Guard would also be cancelled if Kosovo failed to revoke the tariffs.

1.2.Looking Forward

•Government stability: the risk of the Haradinaj government collapsing is rising, particularly given rising US pressure to revoke trade tariffs against Serbia and Bosnia and the recalcitrance of PM Haradinaj over the issue. Key to watch will be any signs that the opposition parties are moving towards cooperation on passing a vote of no confidence[196].

•Trade tariffs: Formal negotiations between Belgrade and Pristina will remain stalled unless the trade tariffs imposed by the latter are removed. Increasing international pressure will come to bear on Kosovo to revoke the tariffs, with a further worsening of relations with key allies likely.

•Kosovo Specialist Chambers: with the Special Prosecutor's Office inviting a steady stream of ex-Kosovo Liberation Army figures to be 'interviewed', it will be important to watch out for the issuing of actual indictments, which could further destabilize the political and security situation in Kosovo.

2.North Macedonia-Election

The elections were the first in North Macedonia after the Prespa agreement on the naming_dispute, signed on 17 June 2018[197]. A referendum was held on 30 September, in which a majority of voters approved the agreement, although turnout was far below the quorum required to validate the result, mainly because of an organized boycott of the Anti-Prespa agreement bloc. The Assembly subsequently approved the change of the country's name to "North Macedonia" on 11 January 2019, and Greece subsequently ratified the agreement and the accession protocol for NATO.

---

195 https://consultancy.birn.eu.com/wp-content/uploads/2019/03/Western-Balkans-Stability-Monitor-March-2019.pdf, pg25 14.10.2019

196 https://consultancy.birn.eu.com/wp-content/uploads/2019/03/Western-Balkans-Stability-Monitor-March-2019.pdf, pg25 14.10.2019

197 Supporter of North Macedonia Name Change Wins Presidency. New York Times, 6 May 2019.

Incumbent President Gjorge Ivanov was a vocal opponent of the name change and refused to sign the laws and amendments on the matter. However, Assembly Speaker Talat Xhaferi claimed that his signature was enough to enforce the changes[198]

The name change had the support of the government coalition formed by the Social Democrats (SDSM) and the ethnic Albanian Democratic Union for Integration. The nationalist VMRO-DPMNE coalition led by Hristijan Mickoski was in favor of NATO integration but against the name change, although the change was approved in the Assembly with at least four VMRO-DPMNE MPs voting in favors[199].

After her nomination, VMRO-DPMNE candidate Gordana Siljanovska-Davkova had promised to initiate a second referendum and restore the old name to the country if she won.[200]

Observation of election (OSCE)

Presidential Election, 21 April and 5 May 2019

Following an invitation to observe the 21 April 2019 presidential election in North Macedonia, and in accordance with its mandate, ODIHR has deployed an Election Observation Mission (EOM).

The ODIHR EOM and the OSCE Mission to Skopje operate separately under their specific mandates.

Long-term Observation

The ODIHR EOM, headed by Corien Jonker, consists of 11 international experts based in Skopje. In addition, 18 long-term observers will be deployed throughout the country from 20 March.[201]

---

[198] *Ivanov: Amnesty is a blackmail for votes for the Prespes Agreement". Independent Balkan News Agency. 28 December 2018.*

[199] *Deputies agree historic name change for Macedonia". France 24. 11 January 2019.*

[200] Polls Open in Macedonia Presidential Elections Balkan Insight, 13 April 2014

[201] Polls Open in Macedonia Presidential Elections Balkan Insight, 13 April 2014

The mission will assess the election for its compliance with OSCE commitments and other international obligations and standards, as well as with national legislation. Observers will follow voter registration, candidate registration, campaign activities, the work of the election administration and relevant state bodies, implementation of the legislative framework, and the resolution of election-related disputes. As part of the observation, the EOM will conduct a comprehensive monitoring of the media.[202]

Election Day

ODIHR will request participating States to second 250 short-term observers for election day. The short-term observers will be deployed throughout the country in multinational teams of two to monitor the opening of polling stations, the voting, the counting of ballots, and the tabulation of results.

The day after the election, ODIHR, together with its parliamentary partners, will issue a statement of preliminary findings and conclusions at a press conference. A final report on the observation of the entire electoral process will be issued approximately two months after the end of the observation mission.

Co-operation with Other Partners

The OSCE Parliamentary Assembly (OSCE PA) and the Parliamentary Assembly of the Council of Europe (PACE) are planning to deploy observer delegations for the election.

Previous Elections

ODIHR has previously observed 17 elections and 2 referenda in the country, most recently the 2018 referendum.

Some data

The election took place in the context of important developments for the country's ambitions for membership in the North Atlantic Treaty Organization (NATO) and the European Union (EU). Following a bilateral agreement with Greece ("Prespa Agreement") in June 2018, and a

---

[202] Polls Open in Macedonia Presidential Elections Balkan Insight, 13 April 2014

consultative referendum in September, the parliament enacted constitutional amendments in January 2019 to change the country's constitutional name in accordance with the agreement. On 6 February 2019, NATO member states signed a protocol on North Macedonia's accession. In the pre-election period, the prime minister publicly highlighted the importance of the democratic conduct of the election in advancing the country's progress towards EU accession and NATO membership. North Macedonia is a Balkan country that has political stability and integration into Euro-Atlantic structures, the political position of the state is moving in the positive direction of political stability, as economic development still remains a problem that many states need to work on stimulating the private sector. Relation between Albanian and Macedonians are good and tis the great hope for two people to live and contribute for state. International Agreement with Greek for name North Macedonia it is great moments. Now North Macedonia is great political position to become part of EU and NATO.

1.2.Electoral System and Legal Framework

The president is directly elected by popular vote under a majoritarian system for a term of five years, with a maximum of two terms. To be elected in the first round, a candidate must receive the votes of a majority of all registered voters.[203] Otherwise, a second round is held within two weeks between the two candidates who received the highest number of votes. The candidate who receives more votes in the second round is elected, provided that there is a turnout of at least 40 per cent of registered voters. Otherwise, the entire election process is repeated. The law does not specify when repeat elections should be held. As previously pointed out by ODIHR and the Council of Europe's Commission for Democracy through Law (Venice Commission),there are no guarantees that a repeat election would enjoy a higher voter turnout, thus the second round turnout requirement may lead to cycles of failed elections.[204]Consideration should be given to

---

[203] As noted in the 2011 ODIHR and Venice Commission Joint Opinion on the Electoral Code, this high threshold (50 per cent of registered voters) is a departure from a more common rule of more than 50 per cent of the valid votes cast in an election.

[204] The 2011 ODIHR and Venice Commission Joint Opinion on the Electoral Code recommended that the threshold requirement in the second round be removed. See also prior ODIHR observation reports in North Macedonia. 9The legal framework also includes, inter alia, the 2004 Law on Political Parties, the 2004 Law on Financing Political Parties, the

reviewing the existing thresholds for presidential elections to minimize the risk of failed elections. The legal framework could be amended to calculate the winning majority in the first round from the number of votes cast, while the second round threshold requirement could be removed. The presidential election is primarily regulated by the 1991 Constitution and the 2006 Electoral Code.9 The country is party to international and regional instruments relevant to the holding of democratic elections.[205] Recent amendments to the Electoral Code in 2018 and 2019 changed the composition of the State Election Commission (SEC), extended its mandate, and provided for reimbursement of paid political advertisements from the state budget. The legal changes were approved by the parliament through a fast-track procedure without, according to ODIHR EOM interlocutors, meaningful consultation with stakeholders.

1.3. Some important matter and concerns:

- All citizens aged at least 18 years as of Election Day are eligible to vote. Contrary to international standards and a prior ODIHR recommendation, persons with disabilities who are deprived of their legal capacity are disenfranchised
- The registration system for in-country voting is passive and continuous, based on information extracted from the civil and other national registers.31 Citizens registered as temporarily residing abroad were included in separate voter lists within the country. They could also actively register for out-of-country voting at polling stations in diplomatic and consular offices.32 While the SEC is responsible for maintaining and updating the voter register, it does not have the capacity to administer the organizational, technical and methodological processing of data, which is performed by the State Statistical Office.
- All citizens have the right to verify their individual data in the voter register in-person or online and to request changes throughout the year. Public scrutiny of the voter list for this election was held between 23 February and 14 March, when the voters were able to

---

1996 Criminal Code, the 2013 Law on Media, and the 2013 Law on Audio and Audiovisual Media Services, as well as instructions of the State Election Commission.

[205] North Macedonia has ratified key international and regional human rights instruments, including the International Covenant on Civil and Political Rights (ICCPR), European Convention on Human Rights (ECHR), United Nations (UN) Convention on the Elimination of All Forms of Discrimination against Women, UN Convention on the Rights of Persons with Disabilities (CRPD) and the UN Convention against Corruption (UNCAC).

verify the data and request changes or corrections in-person in the SEC regional offices.33 According to the SEC, 53,972 voters used this opportunity, including voters who came to sign candidate nomination lists.34 The SEC provided copies of the preliminary voter lists to five parliamentary parties after the conclusion of public scrutiny. Concern over misuse of voters' personal data by political parties to track and pressure voters was voiced by some ODIHR EOM interlocutors.

- To improve the accuracy of the voter lists and to facilitate voters' participation, consideration should be given to extending the period of scrutiny of the voter lists and to bringing the deadline for changes closer to election day. An update of the voter register between rounds could also be considered.

Conditions for candidate to become an elected president :

- According to the Constitution, a citizen aged at least 40 who has been resident in the country for at least 10 of the last 15 years is eligible to stand for the office of president. The latter requirement runs.
- The authorities should reconsider the residency requirement for presidential candidates. Nomination of a presidential candidate must be supported by signatures of 30 members of parliament or at least 10,000 voters. As required by law, voters signed in support of nominees at the premises of SEC regional offices, allowing for direct verification of authenticity of the signatures. In order to facilitate the process, the SEC opened 45 temporary offices in addition to its 34 permanent regional offices. Most ODIHR EOM interlocutors expressed confidence in the practice of signature collection at SEC regional offices, although two complaints were filed to the SEC.
- The Electoral Code stipulates a two-week period for signature collection, which took place between 23 February and 9 March. As previously recommended by ODIHR, voters could sign in support of more than one candidate. Given the considerable number of signatures required to be collected, this time limit is relatively short and has the potential to constrain the inclusiveness of the candidate nomination process.

The Electoral Code stipulates a two-week period for signature collection, which took place between 23 February and 9 March. As previously recommended by ODIHR, voters could sign in support of more than one candidate. Given the considerable number of signatures required to be collected, this time limit is relatively short and has the potential to constrain the inclusiveness of the candidate nomination process. Of the nine prospective candidates who announced their intention to collect voter support signatures, three succeeded in collecting the required number[206]. The SEC received and considered the nomination documents within the legal deadline, and three candidates were registered on 21 March, including one woman and one ethnic-Albanian candidate. According to the SEC, Mr. Pendarovski was supported by 31,729 voter signatures, Mr. Reka by 11,128, and Ms. Siljanovska Davkova by 15,926. Although registered as non-partisan, each of the three candidates was supported by political parties prior to the collection of signatures and registration, and used party symbols for identification on the ballot[207]. Most interlocutors did not raise concerns about the overall inclusiveness of the process.

1.3. CITIZEN AND INTERNATIONAL OBSERVATION

Contributing to the transparency of the electoral process, the Electoral Code provides for observation at all stages by citizen and international observers, as well as representatives of election contestants. The accreditation process for citizen observers is centralized and the accredited organizations are listed on the SEC website, while the responsibility for registration of candidate representatives lies with the MECs. The badges issued to observers and candidate representatives did not indicate their affiliation. In several instances, the IEOM observers saw that candidate representatives were completing their badges themselves[208]. In view of a high number of requests to observe the election, the SEC extended the period for accreditation applications before the first round, and this period

---

[206] PRESIDENTIAL ELECTION21 April and 5 May 2019ODIHR Election Observation Mission Final Report https://www.osce.org/odihr/elections/north-macedonia/428369?download=true,pg24, 20.09.2019

[207]PRESIDENTIAL ELECTION21 April and 5 May 2019ODIHR Election Observation Mission Final Report https://www.osce.org/odihr/elections/north-macedonia/428369?download=true, pg25, 20.09.2019

[208] PRESIDENTIAL ELECTION21 April and 5 May 2019ODIHR Election Observation Mission Final Report https://www.osce.org/odihr/elections/north-macedonia/428369?download=true, pg25,20.09.2019

was further prolonged, with no deadline set, for the run-off[209]. First-round accreditations remained valid in the second round. In an inclusive process, the SEC accredited 3,381 citizen observers and 520 international observers in total for both rounds. Citizen observer groups included CIVIL and Citizens' Association MOST, which also conducted parallel vote tabulation.97 Several organizations of persons with disabilities, such as Inkluziva, also observed the election. On 21 April, voting took place in 3,395 polling stations in the country.98 Election day was calm and the polls were well-administered. The IEOM observed opening in 93 polling stations, voting in 979 polling stations, counting in 87 polling stations and tabulation in 69 MECs.

1.4.ODIHR Recommendations

1. A comprehensive review of electoral legislation should be undertaken to address the shortcomings identified in this and in prior ODIHR reports. Campaign and media rules should regulate the presidential contest and ensure equal opportunities for candidates. Rules for the second round should be clarified. The reform process should be public, inclusive, and carried out sufficiently in advance of the next election.

2. Consideration should be given to reviewing the existing thresholds for presidential elections to minimize the risk of failed elections. The legal framework could be amended to calculate the winning majority in the first round from the number of votes cast, while the second round threshold requirement could be removed.

3.To ensure the stability and professionalism of the election administration, legal provisions should be adopted which clearly establish the composition and length of mandate of a permanent State Election Commission. Essential personnel of the SEC secretariat should be employed on a permanent basis.

4.In a coordinated effort and according to clearly defined responsibilities, the state authorities should continue updating and harmonizing all pertinent registers and databases to provide an accurate basis for the voter register.

5.Continued vigorous efforts should be taken by the authorities to counter any form of pressure on public-sector employees, including clear public statements and written instructions by senior state officials that such pressure will not be tolerated and that no citizen should fear any negative

---

[209] PRESIDENTIAL ELECTION21 April and 5 May 2019ODIHR Election Observation Mission Final Report https://www.osce.org/odihr/elections/north-macedonia/428369?download=true,pg24, 20.09.2019

consequences as a result of supporting or not supporting any candidate or party. Public-sector employees should be actively encouraged to report any instances of pressure, and such cases should be thoroughly investigated and prosecuted, with protection for those who report these cases.

6. The State Audit Office should be mandated to review interim reports and to promptly publish its findings. The deadline for the submission of final reports should not exceed one month after the election. The rules should clarify the reporting structure and requirements, to provide for uniformity of campaign finance reporting.

7. The scope of audits by the State Audit Office (SAO) should ensure comprehensive review of compliance with campaign financing rules, and the SAO should be granted the necessary investigatory powers. To enhance the transparency and effectiveness of campaign finance oversight, the SAO should have adequate resources and technical expertise.

8. The legal framework should be reviewed to eliminate undue restrictions on the right to lodge electoral complaints and appeals, and to provide for effective legal remedies. Decisions and actions of the election administration should be reasoned and subject to timely and effective judicial review.

2.Election in Albania

In November 2018, in line with the Constitution, President Ilir Meta announced the 30 June local elections. Citing concerns for public safety and his constitutional responsibility to protect pluralism, the President revoked the decree on 10 June. On 13 June, parliament passed a resolution declaring the revocation invalid and, on 19 June, it began a procedure, initiated by the Socialist Party (SP), to dismiss the President on grounds of having exceeded his mandate[210]. On 27 June, President Meta announced another decree setting 13 October 2019 as the date for local elections[211]. During this period, the CEC continued preparations to hold the elections on 30 June. The political environment ahead of the elections was polarized and antagonistic. In February, the opposition Democratic Party (DP) and Socialist Movement for Integration (SMI) rescinded their mandates after parliament

[210] The parliament resolution charged among other things that the President had violated the principle of periodicity of elections and the citizens' right to elect.

[211] Unlike the 10 June decree, the presidential decree of 27 June remained unpublished in the Official Gazette, although the publication of acts issued by the President is required by law.

had voted down their initiative on the vetting of politicians. Joined by several smaller parties, the DP and SMI announced that they would not participate in elections until the resignation of Prime Minister Edi Rama (SP leader) and the formation of a transitional government that would organize early parliamentary elections[212]. Regular opposition protests in Tirana, led by the DP, began in February and were often marred by violence and vandalism directed at state institutions, including the offices of the prime minister. The Prime Minister rejected the opposition's demand and, warning against establishing a precedent that would threaten what he described as the "democratic co-existence" of elected governments and their parliamentary opposition, announced that the elections would be held as scheduled. Political crisis, but political parties demonstrated little will overall to engage in constructive co-operation[213]. This antagonism was indicative of the lack of shared responsibility toward the integrity of the electoral process that would transcend party divisions, and, consequently, negatively impacted the right of citizens to take part in government. Following the European Commission's 29 May recommendation to open European Union accession negotiations with Albania, on 18 June the European Council postponed the decision until October 2019. Elections were held for a total of 61 mayors and 1,619 municipal councillors nationwide. Mayors and councils are elected directly for four-year terms. Mayors are elected in first-past-the-post contests and councillors from closed lists under a proportional system. The constituencies for local elections are the territories of the municipalities. There are no specific provisions for the conduct of unopposed elections, and there is no minimum voter turnout requirement for the validation of results. The number of councilors to be elected in each municipality is determined according to its population size and ranges from 15 to 61. To qualify for seat allocation, parties must pass a three per cent threshold of votes cast in the respective municipality, while coalitions must pass a five per cent

---

[212] Unlike the 10 June decree, the presidential decree of 27 June remained unpublished in the Official Gazette, although the publication of acts issued by the President is required by law.

[213] See the general principles of the Council of Europe's European Commission for Democracy through Law (Venice Commission) Parameters on the Relationship between the Parliamentary Majority and the Opposition in a Democracy: A Checklist, CDL-AD(2019)015 (24 June), pp. 7-8.

threshold[214]. Local council mandates are allocated to parties and coalitions according to the d'Hondt method, while the distribution of seats to parties within a coalition is conducted using the Sainte-Laguë method[215].

2.1.CENTRAL ELECTION COMMISSION

The CEC is a permanent body appointed by parliament. By law it is composed of seven members, three each nominated by the parliamentary majority and parliamentary opposition[216] with chairperson elected by parliament through a process of open application. During these elections, the CEC consisted of five members, including the chairperson formally not affiliated with a party, three members nominated by the SP and one by the Republican Party[217]. The DP has not filled its quota of two members since October 2018.The CEC is in charge of the overall conduct of elections. It has a broad mandate and responsibilities, including issuing binding decisions, registering parties and coalitions, training lower level commissions, considering complaints, monitoring campaign finance and accrediting international and citizen observers. The 10 June presidential decree was regarded as void by the majority of CEC members. In municipalities governed by SP mayors, preparations for the elections continued as planned. In almost all municipalities governed by the opposition, the mayors ordered the CEAZs to discontinue preparations and vacate municipal premises. As a result, the CEC had to reallocate more than 200 voting centers as well as a number of CEAZs and BCCs. The opposition's calls on the electorate to boycott the elections, the political bias of municipal authorities and an unbalanced composition of the election administration all negatively affected the public confidence in the electoral process.

2.2.CAMPAIGN ENVIRONMENT

---

[214] An independent candidate obtains a seat in a council if the number of votes for this candidate is greater than the minimal quotient defined for the allocation of seats for parties and coalitions.

[215] When voting for a coalition, a voter chooses one of its constituent parties expressing thereby her or his preference. The number of individual votes for a party within a coalition defines the number of seats allocated to this party out of the total number of seats won by the coalition in a given constituency.

[216] The largest parliamentary majority and the largest opposition party propose two CEC members each. In addition, the next largest parliamentary majority and opposition parties propose one member each.

[217] The current CEC deputy chairperson is the former chairperson, and was nominated to the CEC on the Republican Party quota. He became deputy chairperson as a consequence of a political agreement in 2017.

The campaign, which began on 31 May and lasted until the start of electoral silence on 29 June, was largely invisible. Apart from voter education billboards with materials provided to municipal authorities by the CEC, the ODIHR EOM observed few posters or other signs of imminent elections. Contestants campaigned predominantly in social media, through door-to-door visits and small-scale meetings with voters. There was little face-to-face debate among the candidate.

2.3.CAMPAIGN FINANCE

Electoral campaigns may be financed from public and private resources, including loans. Public funds are allocated to parties for their regular activities based on their results in the last parliamentary elections.[218] Additional public funds are provided for campaign purposes to all parties contesting the elections as an advance, and recalculated after the elections. On 16 May, the parliament allocated ALL 65 million (some EUR 533,000) for these purposes.[219] On 10 June, the CEC divided the sum among the parties contesting the elections in proportion to their results in the last local elections: ALL 41 million went to the SP, and the remainder to 35 other eligible contesting parties. Parties that secure fewer votes than their funding entitlement must repay the difference. Independent candidates are not entitled to public funding. Donations from both citizens and domestic legal entities, including in-kind, are capped at ALL 1 million (EUR 8,200). Contributions above ALL 100,000 must be made through a designated bank account.[220]

RECOMMENDATIONS

These recommendations as contained throughout the text are offered with a view to further enhance the conduct of elections in the Republic of Albania and to support efforts to bring them fully in line with OSCE commitments and other international obligations and standards for

---

[218] An independent candidate obtains a seat in a council if the number of votes for this candidate is greater than the minimal quotient defined for the allocation of seats for parties and coalitions

[219] An independent candidate obtains a seat in a council if the number of votes for this candidate is greater than the minimal quotient defined for the allocation of seats for parties and coalitions

[220] An independent candidate obtains a seat in a council if the number of votes for this candidate is greater than the minimal quotient defined for the allocation of seats for parties and coalitions

democratic elections. These recommendations should be read in conjunction with past ODIHR recommendations that have not yet been addressed. ODIHR stands ready to assist the authorities of the Republic of Albania to further improve the electoral process and to address the recommendations contained in this and previous reports.[221]

1.With a view to strengthen pluralistic democracy, reaffirm the right of citizens to take part in government and demonstrate shared responsibility toward the integrity of the electoral process, political parties and other electoral stakeholders should engage in an open and inclusive dialogue and facilitate electoral reform addressing the recommendations contained in this and prior ODIHR reports. 2.The authorities and political parties should undertake utmost measures to eliminate the long-standing problem of misuse of administrative resources in and between elections. Authorities should issue precise rules that define how public resources may and may not be used for electoral purposes. Further steps should be taken to achieve the de-politicisation of the civil service and ensure that pressure is not applied on voters to attend campaign events or vote in a particular way. 3.Authorities should guarantee the voters' right to a free and secret choice. The voting procedures should be reviewed to ensure the secrecy of the vote and protection against undue influence on voters. The importance of ballot secrecy should be emphasized during the training of election commissions and in voter education materials.

4.In line with previous ODIHR recommendations, in order to enhance public confidence in the electoral process, consideration should be given to alternative formulas for nominating members of election administration, supported by procedural safeguards for their independence.[222]

5.All courts that have a competency in elections should be fully operational during the electoral periods. The independence and the impartiality of the Central Election Commission and the judiciary should be ensured.

6.Law enforcement bodies should investigate all allegations of electoral violations thoroughly, swiftly and in a transparent manner. The government should establish a procedure by which current and prospective public administration employees may report any political pressures brought upon them in connection with obtaining or retaining a position or with work

---

[221] ODIHR stands ready to assist the authorities of the Republic of Albania to further improve the electoral process and to address the recommendations contained in this and previous reports

[222] ODIHR stands ready to assist the authorities of the Republic of Albania to further improve the electoral process and to address the recommendations contained in this and previous reports

performance. Such persons should enjoy the protections currently guaranteed by law to whistle-blowers.

Election Administration

7.Effective measures should be taken to further strengthen the recruitment and training methods of commissioners in order to ensure their professionalism. To enhance the professional capacity of election commissions, the Central Election Commission could offer periodic training and certification of potential commissioners, with the aim of creating a roster of qualified people.

8.To increase the transparency of the work, the Central Election Commission should systematically and in a timely manner publish all decisions on its website.

9.Authorities should take a proactive role ensuring accessibility of voting centres for persons with disabilities. Premises that lack accessibility should be identified well in advance and alternative solutions offered where necessary. Voter Registration

10.Restrictions on the suffrage rights of persons with mental disabilities and non-citizens in local elections should be reconsidered.[223]

Candidate Registration

11.The rules on candidate registration and withdrawals should be formulated precisely and their implementation by the Central Election Commission should be guided by the principle of legal certainty. Electoral Campaign[224]

12.To prevent inflammatory and insulting language during campaign, political parties and electoral contestants could develop and adhere to a common code of conduct. Political parties should strengthen enforcement of their internal ethical codes, foster internal party democracy and ensure that their internal functions respect and promote transparency, equality and non-discrimination..Awareness should be raised about the importance of equal participation of women and men in public and political life, in both

---

[223] ODIHR stands ready to assist the authorities of the Republic of Albania to further improve the electoral process and to address the recommendations contained in this and previous reports

[224] ODIHR stands ready to assist the authorities of the Republic of Albania to further improve the electoral process and to address the recommendations contained in this and previous reports

urban and rural areas, and with a particular emphasis on the role of women within political parties and electoral processes. [225]
Republic of Albania Page: 28 Local Elections[226], 30 June 2019 ODIHR Election Observation Campaign Finance14.Consideration should be given to reviewing the law to ensure that the CEC has the appropriate powers and procedures to effectively oversee and enforce party and campaign finance rules. Media15.The independence of the media regulator and public broadcaster should be further strengthened through measures that prevent conflict of interest. Senior management positions at the public broadcaster should not be accessible to people with clear political affiliation.[227]

16.The audiovisual media law should be amended to effectively limit concentration of media ownership in the broadcast sector.

17.The Electoral Code should be amended to guarantee equal access to the media for all contesting parties in all types of editorial programming and to allow all contestants to purchase advertising space under equal conditions. Additional considerations could be given to allocating a certain amount of free time equally to all contestants.

18.The responsibilities of the MMB should be clearly defined. The MMB should adopt a monitoring methodology in a timely manner, publish without delay its media monitoring reports, as well as decisions and other types of letters and requests to the media. The MMB should be allotted adequate resources for more detailed media monitoring, including of regional broadcasters.

19.Legislation should be amended to ensure that the media are able to independently cover activities of electoral contestants with a view to limit the use of party produced content in news programming and avoid

[225] ODIHR stands ready to assist the authorities of the Republic of Albania to further improve the electoral process and to address the recommendations contained in this and previous reports

[226] ODIHR stands ready to assist the authorities of the Republic of Albania to further improve the electoral process and to address the recommendations contained in this and previous reports

[227] ODIHR stands ready to assist the authorities of the Republic of Albania to further improve the electoral process and to address the recommendations contained in this and previous reports

misleading voters. Whenever content produced by political parties is used by the media, it should be clearly labelled.

Complaints and Appeals

20.In order to ensure transparency of electoral dispute resolution outcomes, all decisions of the Electoral College could be published promptly and be accessible to all.[228]

Election in Montenegro
POLITICAL CONTEXT

On 19 January 2018, the president of parliament called the presidential election for 15 April. According to the Constitution the legislative powers are exercised by the parliament, the executive powers by the Government and the judicial by courts[229].This was the third presidential election since independence in 2006. The incumbent president, Filip Vujanović, could not run for re-election. In the most recent 2016 parliamentary elections, the Democratic Party of Socialists (DPS) won 36 out of 81 seats and, with the support of four other parties, maintained the majority it has enjoyed since 1991.3 Following the elections, opposition parties refused to accept the results and initiated a parliamentary boycott, which considerably limited the political dialogue and the versight of government work[230]. In December 2017, the boycott impeded the adoption of several amendments to the electoral framework aimed at addressing previous ODIHR recommendations. After the calling of the election, opposition parties held negotiations aimed at reaching a consensus on a joint presidential candidate. Notwithstanding the calls for unity, the Social Democratic Party (SDP) and United Montenegro (UCG) left the talks, and the opposition went fragmented to the election. On 5 March, SDP announced their own

[228] ODIHR stands ready to assist the authorities of the Republic of Albania to further improve the electoral process and to address the recommendations contained in this and previous reports

[229] The President represents the country abroad, proposes candidates for prime minister, president and judges of the Constitutional Court and is supreme commander of the army.

[230] Democratic Front (DF), Democratic Montenegro (DCG), Social Democratic Party (SDP), Socialist People's Party (SNP), Demos, and United Reform Action (URA), with a combined total of 39 seats supported the boycott. In December 2017, 20 members from DF and the newly created United Montenegro (UCG) – a split from Demos– returned to the parliament although they do not participate in the legislative process

candidate, and UCG decided to support the joint candidate announced on 9 March by Democratic Front (DF), Democratic Montenegro (DCG), United Reform Action (URA) and Socialist People's Party (SNP).The election took place against the background of renewed expectations for accession to the European Union (EU), continued debates on NATO membership, and ongoing discussions on the international alignment of the country. The general security situation became a campaign issue after several non-election related violent incidents occurred in various locations across the country.

VOTER REGISTRATION

Voter registration is passive. The voter list is permanent and centrally maintained by the Ministry of Interior (MoI) based on information from four different registers[231].

18 by election day have the right to vote. Those declared legally incapacitated by a court decision are deprived of the right to vote, a restriction that is at odds with OSCE commitments and other international obligations and standards. The Constitution guarantees citizens the right to vote if they have resided in the country for two years prior to election day, and the election law further restricts the right to vote only to those who were residents for the last two years immediately before election day[232]. ODIHR and the Venice Commission have previously criticized the residency requirement as not being in line with international standards[233].The residency and legal competence requirements for voting should be reviewed in line with the international obligations and good practice to allow for broader participation in the elections. Public scrutiny of the voter list started on 21 January and ended on 31 March. During this period, citizens could make requests for corrections in their data on the MoI website or in person at municipal offices.27 A total of 12,282 requests for corrections were made including 1,353 requests to change residence. Political parties and accredited citizen observer groups have the right to inspect the voter lists at the office of the MoI upon request. On 2 April, the Centre for Democratic Transition (CDT) requested that the MoI check a

---

[231] Registers for citizenship, residence, birth and death.

[232] See previous ODIHR reports on Montenegro. Paragraph I.1.1.c.iii of the Code of Good Practice states that a length of residence requirement may be imposed on nationals solely for local or regional elections. See also ODIHR and Venice Commission 2011 Joint Opinion on the Draft Law on amendments to the law on Election of Councillors and Members of Parliament.

[233] Individuals or their authorized representatives can submit requests for corrections.

separate fingerprint database against the data in the voter list to determine if a fingerprint could be linked to several identification documents, which would allow for multiple voting. The MoI ran a crosscheck between the databases and 89 voters' fingerprints were linked to several identification documents. According to the MoI, the voters were allowed to vote and the investigation is ongoing. The voter list was closed 10 days before election day and the SEC announced that the total number of voters was 532,599.

CANDIDATE REGISTRATION

Voters with residence in the country for at least 10 of the last 15 years are eligible to stand. Political parties and citizens' groups nominating presidential candidates must collect supporting signatures from at least 1.5 per cent of the electorate. This is not in line with established good practice which states that required signatures should not exceed one per cent of the electorate. Despite previous ODIHR recommendations, the election law still requires each voter to sign in support of only one presidential candidate which could limit political pluralism.As previously recommended, consideration could be given to remove the restriction to sign in support of only one candidate and to limit the number of support signatures required to stand for office to no more than one per cent of the total electorate. The candidate registration process started on 19 January and ended on 26 March. In an attempt to improve transparency, on 12 March the SEC introduced an online application allowing voters to check if their names appeared on a signature support list. A number of media and some candidates criticized the SEC because the application was introduced after three candidates had already been registered. On 16 March, a candidate requested the SEC to provide him with the official decision on development and use of the application. The SEC rejected the request as, despite a public announcement by the SEC, there was no written decision or instructions on the use of the application. Numerous voters discovered through the SEC online application that their signatures were forged in support of some candidates. Over 1,000 complaints alleging forged signatures were filed with the prosecutor's office. In addition, voters' requests to have their personal data deleted from the SEC database or to have their signatures withdrawn were rejected. (See Complaints and Appeals)The legal framework does not contain sanctions for falsification of documentation for candidacy registration, nor does it detail the procedure the SEC should follow in such a situation. The lack of legal clarity and the late introduction of the application was at odds with international good practice which requires that the rules for verification of signatures be applied fairly and equally to all parties.The law should be amended to include clear instructions for signature verification, reasonable timeframe for the review of signatures and adequate sanctions for violations. Seven candidates, six men and one woman, ran for this election. The candidate registration, although impaired by some procedural challenges that cast doubts on the process, was inclusive and the SEC registered all candidates who submitted nomination documents.

ELECTION CAMPAIGN

During the campaign, fundamental freedoms of assembly, movement and association were respected, although the candidate nominated by the governing party held an institutional advantage. The authorities granted access to public places on an equal basis, and contestants were able to campaign without restrictions. A number of ODIHR EOM interlocutors viewed the upcoming local elections as more important than the presidential election. Most candidates started campaigning three weeks before election day and their activities were generally low-key. The campaign ended 24 hours before election day. Candidates could start campaigning once their registration was approved by the SEC. However, the law does not determine when the electoral campaign officially begins, thus causing confusion as to when campaign regulations apply. This lack of definition blurs the timeframe for the oversight of campaign finance, for imposing restrictions on public officials for campaigning, or for granting equal access of candidates to purchase advertisements on private media. Furthermore, it allows for early campaigning, in the absence of a sanctioning mechanism. As previously recommended, consideration should be given to amending the election law to clearly define when the official campaign period starts.

CAMPAIGN FINANCING

The Law on Financing of Political Entities and Election Campaigns provides for public and private funding of election campaigns[234]. Candidates can

[234] The state allocated EUR 594,999 of public funds for the campaign. Twenty per cent of the public funding was distributed equally among all candidates but the funds were not transferred within the legal deadline. The remaining 80 per cent is proportionally distributed among the candidates who receive more than 3 per cent of votes after submission of the final reports. Only three candidates are entitled to receive the second instalment

receive monetary and in-kind donations from individuals. and legal entities. The limit for contributions from individuals is EUR 2,000 and from legal entities EUR 10,000. Contributions from anonymous donors, trade unions, religious communities, non-governmental and state-funded organizations, as well as foreign sources are forbidden. There is no distinction between contributions received from political parties and other legal entities. Some candidates received loans from parties, despite the legal restriction on credits from other sources than financial institutions. All transactions must be conducted through a dedicated account, but the law does not clearly define when it has to be opened. Gaps and ambiguities in the law regarding the use of loans and party resources to finance the election campaign should be addressed. The timeframe for opening the campaign bank account could also be installed by the law. The Agency for Prevention of Corruption (APC) is tasked with the overall supervision of campaign finance regulations and can initiate sanctioning proceedings for breaches. It conducts monitoring and field inspections during the campaign, but the control remains formalistic and limited due to the limited capacities, as the review is primarily based on the documentation submitted by the candidates. The APC failed to proactively react to breaches of campaign finance regulations and did not issue warnings or initiate sanctioning procedure against candidates reporting incorrect figures on expenditure. Further measures could be taken to guarantee independence and strengthen the capacities of the APC with a view to ensure effective implementation of the law. APC should develop sound methodology for inspection of financial activities of the contestants during the campaign. All candidates reported on their personal finances, including income and property, within 15 days of their registration to the APC. Reports on donations were submitted in a timely manner every 15 days, and interim reports on expenses were filed five days prior to election day. APC published the interim reports online, but poor quality scanned copies impeded a proper disclosure of the data and curtailed transparency. Final reports were submitted 30 days after the election. Candidates received private donations predominantly from individuals, and to a lesser amount from legal entities, but did not report in-kind donations. Contestants mostly spent the funds on media advertisement, billboards, and goods and services for organizing public events. In general, provided information lacked clarity and consistency.

CITIZEN AND INTERNATIONAL OBSERVERS

The legal framework provides for observation by citizen and international observers. The SEC accredited 333 international (a number which includes some 130 local supporting staff) and 1,682 citizen observers. The Centre for Monitoring and Research (CEMI) deployed some 1,300 observers on election day and conducted parallel vote tabulation (PVT) with a sample of approximately 1,100 polling stations. The CDT observed the work of the SEC, the candidate registration process, deployed approximately 300 observers on election day and also conducted a PVT. Network for Affirmation of NGO Sector (MANS) focused mainly on monitoring campaign finance while the Centre for Civic Education (CCE) conducted media monitoring.

RECOMMENDATIONS

These recommendations as contained throughout the text are offered with a view to further enhance the conduct of elections in Montenegro and to support efforts to bring them fully in line with OSCE commitments and other international obligations and standards for democratic elections. These recommendations should be read in conjunction with past ODIHR recommendations that have not yet been addressed. The ODIHR stands ready to assist the authorities of Montenegro to further improve the electoral process and to address the recommendations contained in this and previous reports.

A.PRIORITY RECOMMENDATIONS

1.Comprehensive and inclusive review of the electoral legal framework should be considered to regulate all key aspects of the election process, address omissions and to harmonize provisions from different election laws to avoid legal collision. All amendments should be adopted in broad and inclusive public consultation well in advance of the next election.

2.The authorities should promptly and thoroughly investigate all allegations of electoral violations and, in conjunction with the political parties, should undertake measures to discourage vote-buying and to prevent pressure on citizens to participate in the campaign events or to influence their vote.

3.To increase transparency and to earn public trust, SEC should allow access of media to all its meetings. The SEC and MECs should publish all relevant documents and decisions on their websites in a timely manner.

4.Election administration and judiciary should ensure meaningful, substantive and impartial consideration of complaints in line with clear and transparent legal procedures. Institutions dealing with dispute resolution should be sufficiently empowered to implement necessary control over the electoral process in accordance with clearly defined jurisdiction rules

.5.The law should be amended to include clear instructions for signature verification, reasonable timeframe for the review of signatures and adequate sanctions for violations.
6.The SEC could consider revising election day procedures and develop clear tabulation procedures to enhance consistency in the reporting of results, and ensure the transparency and accountability of the process.
7.To foster the independence of the RTCG and the AEM, council's members should be protected from undue influence from politics, and early dismissals should be permitted only in limited circumstances.

8.Authorities should firmly condemn any attacks against journalists and foster measures to protect journalists and prevent impunity, including independent, speedy, effective investigations, and detailed and systematic data collection on threats against journalists.

B.OTHER RECOMMENDATIONS

Election Administration
9.In order to ensure consistency, the SEC should exercise its legal authority to promulgate clear and consistent instructions and regulations to address gaps in the electoral law The SEC should operate and adopt its decisions with the legally required quorum. Additional measures to safeguard integrity, impartiality and professionalism of the election administration could be taken to avoid politicization of decision-making. The role of authorized representatives at all levels of election administration needs to be clarified and consideration given to limiting their involvement in decision-making[235].Voter Registration11.The residency and legal competence requirements for voting should be reviewed in line with the international obligations and good practice to allow for broader participation in the elections.Candidate Registration 12.As previously recommended, consideration could be given to remove the restriction to sign in support of only one candidate and to limit the number of support

[235]OSCE, Election Administration, observatory mission-Recommendation, SEC,2018

signatures required to stand for office to no more than one per cent of the total electorate.Election Campaign13.As previously recommended, consideration should be given to amending the election law to clearly define when the official campaign period starts.

Campaign Finance

14.Gaps and ambiguities in the law regarding the use of loans and party resources to finance the election campaign should be addressed. The timeframe for opening the campaign bank account could also be installed by the law.

15.Further measures could be taken to guarantee independence and strengthen the capacities of the APC with a view to ensure effective implementation of the law. APC should develop sound methodology for inspection of financial activities of the contestants during the campaign.

16.The reporting templates should be itemized to provide for a clear distinction between different categories of expenses, including types of advertisements and to be published in a user-friendly format. Consideration could be given to developing guidelines on calculation of in-kind contributions.

Media

17.Whilst public support for the media can enhance pluralism, a transparent and non-discriminatory allocation of state advertising funds should be required. Alternative forms of indirect subsidies, such as tax benefits, or direct subsidies based on objective criteria and conditions may be considered.

18.Consideration could be given to granting the AEM more effective enforcement mechanisms to include intermediate financial sanctions, commensurate with the gravity of the offence committed. To avoid overlapping jurisdiction and ensure effective remedies, the AEM should be the only body responsible for supervising broadcasters during the elections.

19.The authorities could consider imposing a limit on the amount of paid political advertising which could contribute to more balanced level playing field. Media should offer equivalent rates to all candidates, avoiding negotiations on the price, and the rates should be made public before the election campaign.

Complaints and Appeals

20. Consideration could be given to setting specific expedited time limits for investigation and adjudication of election related complaints in misdemeanor and criminal procedure. Voting, **Counting and Tabulation**

21. To encourage equal participation of persons with disabilities in elections, the election administration and other relevant institutions should take further measures to improve the accessibility of polling stations.
22.To increase the transparency in the election process, the election day procedures could be revised to include posting copy of results protocols outside the premises of the polling stations and to publish them online.

3.Serbia political development and election

Among the Western Balkan countries aspiring to EU membership, Serbia is seen as a frontrunner in terms of its democratic institutions, level of economic development and overall readiness for accession[236]. However, in November 2018 opposition politician, Borko Stefanović, was beaten up by thugs, triggering a wave of protests that has spread across the country. Week after week, thousands have taken to the streets, accusing Serbian president, Aleksandar Vučić, and his Serbian Progressive Party (SNS) of authoritarian rule, attacks on independent media, electoral fraud and corruption[237].
Although the protests only started recently, they highlight worrying longer-term trends. Press freedom has been in decline for several years, particularly since Vučić became prime minister in 2014. A large part of the media is now controlled either directly by the state or by pro-SNS figures. Independent journalists face threats and even violence, and perpetrators are rarely convicted. In the National Assembly, the governing coalition uses its parliamentary majority to systematically block meaningful discussions of legislative proposals. In protest, the opposition started a boycott of plenary debates in February 2019[238].
The tone of verbal attacks by SNS politicians and their allies on independent media, the political opposition and civil society is often virulent. Criticizing government policy is framed as betrayal of Serbian interests. The aim seems to be to marginalize critical voices while concentrating power in the hands of the SNS-led government. Elected to the mainly ceremonial role of president in 2017, Vučić nevertheless remains the dominant figure[239].

---

[236] European Parliament, Serbia at risk of authoritarianism? Briefing,2019
[237] European Parliament, Serbia at risk of authoritarianism? Briefing,2019
[238] European Parliament, Serbia at risk of authoritarianism? Briefing,2019
[239] European Parliament, Serbia at risk of authoritarianism? Briefing,2019

If Serbia's drift towards authoritarianism continues, it could become a major obstacle to EU accession, for which 2025 has been mentioned as a possible date. Some concern in Serbia:

- Anti- and pro-government rallies spread across Serbia
- Media freedom in decline
- Excessive concentration of political Power
- Elections are not fully free and fair Judicial reforms are lagging behind
- Civil society under attack
- Serbia's EU accession process
-

Excessive concentration of political power

Political power in the hands of Vučić According to Serbia's Constitution, executive power is vested in the government, led by the prime minister; the president's role is mainly ceremonial[240]. Vučić served as prime minister twice, from 2014 to 2016, and again (after calling early elections) from 2016 to 2017, when he was elected president. Vučić himself has pointed out that the constitutional powers he wields as president are 'not even one-tenth' those of the prime minister. His replacement, Ana Brnabić, was an innovative choice, being both the first woman and first openly gay person in the position.However, in practice Vučić's position as leader of the dominant SNS party gives him control of the parliamentary majority, and therefore also of the government[241]. Brnabić lacks her own power base and remains a loyal follower of the president[242]. For Serbs, Vučić continues to embody executive power: he is the country's most popular politician and the one mentioned most frequently in the media; the SNS party list in the 2018 Belgrade local election bore his name; for the 'one in five million' protestors, Vučić is the object of their discontent[243]. In Russia, Vladimir Putin remained the country's undisputed leader, despite the switch of roles with Dmitry Medvedev between 2008 and 2012; Serbia risks going in a similar direction, with constitutional

[240] European Parliament, Serbia at risk of authoritarianism? Briefing,2019
[241] European Parliament, Serbia at risk of authoritarianism? Briefing,2019
[242] European Parliament, Serbia at risk of authoritarianism? Briefing,2019
[243] European Parliament, Serbia at risk of authoritarianism? Briefing,2019

provisions becoming irrelevant compared to the de facto power concentrated in the person of Vučić[244].

The opposition is increasingly weak

Weak and divided, Serbia's opposition has not benefited from the current wave of public protests. Although opposition politicians play a prominent role in 'one in five million' demonstrations, massive public support reflects grassroots discontent with Vučić than support for his rivals. In February 2019, the opposition Alliance for Serbia coalition leaders signed an Agreement with the People in response to the protests, but their text offers few new ideas. With the political leanings of Alliance parties ranging from left-wing to far-right, there is no clarity on which policy changes would come with a future government led by them. In opinion polls from the same month, a mere 15 % of respondents declared an intention to vote for the Alliance, compared to around 50 % for Vučić's SNS, not including its current coalition partners. Even among protestors, fewer than half identify with any of the opposition parties.

Elections are not fully free and fair

OSCE/ODIHR observers at the 2016 parliamentary and 2017 presidential elections – won respectively by the SNS-led coalition and Vučić – concluded that both polls offered voters a genuine choice of candidates[245]. However, they also noted 'credible allegations' of practices such as vote-buying (in the form of offers of free food and health care, or a 'Bulgarian train', in which voters are bribed to cast pre-prepared ballot papers); there were also concerns about the accuracy of voter lists. Observers from Serbian civil society noted similar problems during the March 2018 Belgrade City Assembly elections and December 2018 local elections in Lučani[246]. Public trust in electoral processes has been correspondingly undermined: in an October 2018 survey, 33 % of respondents believed that severe irregularities had at least occasionally compromised election results.Given that the results of the 2016 and 2017 elections were broadly in line with opinion polls, irregularities

[244] European Parliament, Serbia at risk of authoritarianism? Briefing,2019
[245] European Parliament, Serbia at risk of authoritarianism? Briefing,2019
[246] European Parliament, Serbia at risk of authoritarianism? Briefing,2019

on the day of the vote are likely to have had only a marginal effect. A bigger concern is abuse by Vučić and his party of their dominant position in the then pre-election period[247]. Apart from the media bias already mentioned, there were also cases in which SNS incumbent candidates abused administrative resources and their official functions for campaign purposes (for example, hosting SNS campaign events on municipal premises, or distributing campaign leaflets during official visits by government ministers). Some civil servants and private-sector employees were reportedly pressured to take part in SNS rallies[248]. The frequently used power to call early elections with just 45 days' notice (as happened in 2014 and 2016; now, Vučić says he is considering a further snap poll in June 2019), gives incumbents a further advantage[249]. OSCE/ODIHR reports note that most of their previous recommendations, designed to address such issues, have not been followed[250].

3.1.Judicial reforms are lagging behind

Critics of Serbia's legal system, including judges themselves, argue that it is failing to deliver effective justice. Political interference and underfinancing are among the many problems. There is a huge backlog of cases, some of which drag on for years or are never heard due to exceeding the statute of limitations, resulting in impunity[251]. The European Commission's 2018 report[252] on Serbia notes some improvements; though the judiciary is still inefficient, its 2018 budget has increased nearly 9 % year-on-year. EU funding (€93 million for the rule of law in Serbia since 2006) has helped to clear some of the backlog by bringing in extra administrative staff. Other issues require deeper changes. Under Serbia's 2006 Constitution, most members of the High Judicial Council, which oversees judges and courts, are elected by the National Assembly – an arrangement the Council of Europe's Venice Commission described as 'a recipe for the politicization of the judiciary'[253]. Reforms undertaken as part of

---

[247] European Parliament, Serbia at risk of authoritarianism? Briefing,2019

[248] European Parliament, Serbia at risk of authoritarianism? Briefing,2019

[249] Blic, Serbian President Vucic, pg.3,Beograd June 2019

[250] European Parliament, Serbia at risk of authoritarianism? Briefing,2019

[251] European Parliament, Serbia at risk of authoritarianism? Briefing,2019

[252]The European Commission's 2018 report

[253] European Parliament, Serbia at risk of authoritarianism? Briefing,2019

the country's EU accession process aim to make courts more independent. Constitutional amendments submitted to the National Assembly in November 2018envisage changes to the composition of the High Judicial Council[254]. However, the proposed changes are highly contested, with judges and civil-society organizations arguing that the constitutional amendments proposed by the Ministry of Justice do not fully address the issue of judicial independence; even if fewer members of the Council are now elected by the National Assembly, in practice the parliamentary majority still retains considerable influence over it[255]. Judicial independence also has to do with political culture. Serbian politicians habitually comment on ongoing cases and criticize the work of the courts – a practice that looks set to continue, regardless of constitutional changes.

Conclusion

- Kosovo should establish the Assembly and the Government as soon as possible after the extraordinary elections. Kosovo must abolish taxes to resume Kosovo-Serbia dialogue Kosovo must improve the rule of law in justice by adopting the Vetting Act. An independent commission consisting of the KJC and the KPC with EU assistance must implement the law on vetting in the judiciary. Kosovo should be enabled by the EU visa liberalization as soon as possible.Kosovo needs comprehensive reform, with the most important sectors remaining: the economy, law and order, higher education, health protection, social reform.The new government has to deal with sectorial issues mentioned otherwise frustration will be even greater for the citizens. Kosovo needs a new political generation, so with young people aged 35-45 years, the older political generation in Kosovo is considered corrupt, nepotism and unable to make a difference in the lives of citizens. Kosovo must show a clear will to fight corruption. Kosovo should make electoral reform as soon as possible. The proportional system should be changed to half majority.

[254] European Parliament, Serbia at risk of authoritarianism? Briefing,2019
[255]European Parliament, Serbia at risk of authoritarianism? Briefing,2019

- Kosovo and Serbia must find a solution to normalize relations. Kosovo and Serbia must agree on a solution model. Kosovo must maintain its territorial integrity and sovereignty throughout its territory.Dialogue between the two countries should be conducted unconditionally.The Kosovo-Serbia rapprochement agreement should happen as soon as possible. Macedonia should make electoral reform based on EU recommendations. Macedonia needs a law enacted for the state prosecutor and should improve the performance of the judiciary.Macedonia could soon open accession negotiations with the EU. Albania needs to improve the functioning of law and order that remains the main problem and to fight corruption. Political parties in Albania need to become more aware of creating a stable political climate in the country and to attract foreign investors to invest in Albania.Serbia must continue reforms in the sectorial state and build a democratically acceptable system,Serbia should also work on electoral reform and revise its electoral system. Serbia must create new democratic parameters, and parties in Serbia must work together to build a peaceful policy in the Western Balkans. Serbia should find the model of solution for normalization of relations with Kosovo as soon as possible, otherwise Serbia cannot open negotiations for EU membership

- Montenegro should continue its EU integration efforts and also make efforts to improve the rule of law and order.

- Kosovo needs a deep electoral reform, to change the electoral system, the number of constituencies; Kosovo needs a new electoral system that should be semi-majority. Also Albania and Macedonia, Mlaii Zi and Serbia, should are more efficient and meet high democratic criteria in the electoral process. The Western Balkans is highly politicized and this is negatively affecting the choices and the development of democratic circumstances in these countries.

Literature :

- Balkan Insight,October,2019

- Blerim Burjani, Krizat Nderkombetare, Prishtine, 2011

- Central election Commission

- European Parliament, Serbia at risk of authoritarianism? Briefing
- EU observers in election, 6 October 2019
- Euonews: Opposition parties overturn Kosovo politics with election victory,October, 2019
- Kosovo Policy , Institute of Kosovo for Policy Development (IKPD),Pristina, 2010
- Florian Bieber, professor for Southeast European History and Politics at the University of Graz and Coordinator of the Balkans in Europe Policy,2019
- Kosovo Election 2019, Radio Free Europe, https://www.rferl.org/z/679,10.11.2019,Western-Balkans-Stability-Monitor-March-2019
- Kosovo Voters Want a New Future, but Old Problems Linger
- Kosovan parliamentary election, https://en.wikipedia.org/wiki/2021_Kosovan_parliamentary_election
- Kosovo Snap Election –liveblog, https://balkaninsight.com/2021/02/14/kosovo-snap-elections-2021-live-blog/
- In Kosovo, an electoral earthquake, https://emerging-europe.com/tag/kosovo-parliamentary-election-2021/
- NewYork Timeshttps://www.nytimes.com/2019/10/06/world/europe/kosovo-election-haradinaj-osmani.html,6 October,2019
- Kosovo leftist declares victory after election https: // www.dw.com

  /en/kosovo-leftist-kurti-declares-victory-after-election/a-56563753
-
- Koha Vision, 6 October, 2019

- Klan Kosova, 6 October , 2019
- RTK,6 October, 2019
- OSCE, Election Administration, observatory mission-Recommendation, SEC,2018
- Blerim Burjani, Electoral Reform, Institute of Kosovo for Policy Development (IKPD), Pristina,2014
- Blerim Burjani, Interpretation of Law, Institute of Kosovo for Policy Development (IKPD),, Pristina, 2011
- Douche Welle , Kosovo: The final results of the elections are announced, Douche Welle
- Council of Europe, Observation Mission KOSOVO, General Election, October 2004
- Law on General Elections of Republic of Kosovo
- .Law on Local Election Of Republic Kosovo
- Law on Constitutional Court of Slovenia
- Law on Constitutional Court of Croatia
- Law on Constitutional Court of Montenegro
- Law on Constitutional Court of Serbia
- ZGJEDHJET E PARAKOHSHME PËR KUVENDIN E REPUBLIKËS SË KOSOVËS 2019, https://www.kqz-ks.org/zgjedhjet-e-pergjithshme/zgjedhjet-per-kuvend-te-kosoves-2019/ezhguesit
- .Vezhguesit e zgjedhjeve , https://www.kqz-ks.org/zgjedhjet-e-pergjithshme/zgjedhjet-per-kuvend-te-kosoves-2019/
- . Raporti I Vezhgimit te Zgjedhjeve, Zgjedhjet për Kuvendin e Kosovës, http://demokracianeveprim.org/wp-content/uploads/2019/12/DnV_RAPORTI-I-V%C3%8BZHGIMIT-T%C3%8B-ZGJEDHJEVE.pdf,2019

- **Rezultatet preliminare të zgjedhjeve - VV e para** **https://www.dw.com/sq/rezultatet-preliminare-t%C3%AB-zgjedhjeve-vv-e-para/a-50718777**
- **Zyra e OSBE-së për Institucione Demokratike dhe të Drejtat e Njeriut Misioni për Vëzhgimin e Zgjedhjeve Republika e Maqedonisë së Veriut Zgjedhjet e parakohshme parlamentare, 12 prill 2020 RAPORT I PËRKOHSHËM 3 - 31 mars 2020**,https://www.osce.org/files/f/documents/2/3/451369.pdf**15.**
- .Misioni I Bashkimit Evropian per Vezhgimin e Zgjedhjeve ,Raporti Perfundimtar ,Kosove 2014
- **Manual për Ndjekjen e Zbatimit të Rekomandimeve për Zgjedhjet**

-Key findings of th 2020 Report on Kosovo,https: //ec.europa.eu /commission/presscorner/detail/en/COUNTRY_20_1797

- .Support to Elections in the Western Balkans,

OSCE/ ODIR,https://www.osce.org/files/f/documents/4/9/383574.pdf,

- **KOSOVO* MAYORAL AND MUNICIPAL ASSEMBLY ELECTIONS, EUROPEAN UNION ELECTION OBSERVATION MISSION , FINAL REPORT, 22 OCTOBER 2017**
- EU Election Observation Mission Report Mentions KWN's Campaign . https://womensnetwork.org/eu-election-observation-mission-report-mentions-kwns-campaign/
- **The Case of Kosovo: From "International Statebuilding" to an "Internationally Supervised and Independent Country"**https://www.cairn.info/revue-l-europe-en-formation-2008-3-page-189.htm
- **ELECTORAL AND PARTY SYSTEM IN KOSOVO A PERSPECTIVE OF INTERNAL PARTY DEMOCRACY DEVELOPMENT**
- The International Foundation for Electoral Systems (IFES) , SELECTING A MODEL FOR ELECTION ADMINISTRATION IN KOSOVO: CONCLUSIONS & RECOMMENDATIONS FROM DISCUSSION FORUM AND CONFERENCE HELD ON 1-2 AND 16 FEBRUARY 2002
- The International Foundation for Electoral Systems (IFES) , Supporting the CECandECAP,https://www.ifes.org/kosovo?type%5Belection_faq%5D=election_faq&type%5Belection_material%5D=election_material&type%5Bmultimedia%5D=multimedia&type%5Bnews_and_updates%5D=news_and_updates&type%5Bpublication%5D=publication&type%5Bsurvey%5D=survey&page=6
- Bjørg Hope Galtung, KOSOVO: ASSEMBLY ELECTIONS OCTOBER 2004, Report.

- Opposition party Vetëvendosje marks victory in Kosovo's general election,https://europeanwesternbalkans.com/2021/02/17/opposition-party-vetevendosje-marks-victory-in-kosovos-general-election/
-
- United Nations,Recent Kosovo Election Marks Most Significant Change to Political Landscape in 12 Years, Special Representative Tells Security Council, https://www.un.org/press/en/2019/sc14008.doc.htm
- NDI,Kosovo Public Opinion Poll 2020, https: //www.ndi.org /publications/ndi-kosovo-public-opinion-poll-2020
- Beáta Huszka.The power of perspective: Why EU membership still matters in the Western Balkans
- Laura Wise and Timofey Agarin, **European style electoral politics in an ethnically divided society. The case of Kosovo, https: //www. degruyter.com /view/journals /soeu/65/1/article-p99.xml**
- EUROPEAN UNION ELECTION OBSERVATION MISSION TO KOSOVO FOR EARLY PARLIAMENTARY ELECTIONS, POSSIBLE TENTATIVE ELECTION DATES 22 OR 29 SEPTEMBER, OR 06 OCTOBER 201929.
- Elton Tota.EU recommendations on the future elections in Kosovo, https://balkaneu.com/eu-recommendations-on-the-future-elections-in-kosovo/, 12/09/2017

- Elton Tota.EU recommendations on the future elections in Kosovo, https://balkaneu.com/eu-recommendations-on-the-future-elections-in-kosovo/, 12/09/2017

Blerim Burjani was born in Pristina, in capital city of state of Kosovo. Primary and secondary school finish at his birthplace. Law Faculty in the University of Pristina general direction . Magistrates studies at the Law Faculty of the University of Pristina. Until now hold a series of public functions such is Political Adviser to the Minister of Labour and Social Welfare, Political Advisor in the Ministry of Trade and Industry, Representatives of the Government of Kosovo in CEFTA, the former member of the CEC. Blerim has experience 19 years in high education as a lecturer professor at the Business College, was a professor in the College and University of Pristina ,College "Dardania" and "FAMA". In public opinion is known as an expert in development policies and political analyst and executive director of the Kosovo Institute for Development Policy. He has worked for a range of local and international organizations as follows: Council of Europe, KIPA, Human Dynamic in Vienna (Austria), B & S Strategy in Europe, World Bank, UNDP,USAID/RIINVEST, ECMI. He speaks and writes in two international languages: English and Spanish. He lives in Pristina. Books published by author:

- The Free Press Society and Democratization (2000)
- Independent Judiciary (2002)
- Independent Judiciary and Human Rights (2004)
- Local administration (2006)
- Human Rights in Kosovo (2008)
- Poor and marginalized groups(2017)
- The State Emergency Situation (2013)
- International Crisis (2010)
- Interpretation of Law (2011)
- Electoral Reform (2014)
- Concept for Kosovo Foreign Policy (2018)
- Final Agreement For Normalization of Kosovo-Serbia Relations: Possible or impossible final agreement for normalization of Kosovo-Serbia relations (2018)
- Right or Left Political Parties Orientations in Western Balkan
- Judicial Independence in the Western Balkans

- Local Self-government in Kosovo (2018)
- EMPLYMENT, SOCIAL AND HEALTH PROTECTION
- Youth Policy (2019)
- ELECTION IN WESTERN BALKAN AND POLITICAL DVELOPMENT(2019)

Printed by Books on Demand GmbH, Norderstedt / Germany